CHILI DAWGS ALWAYS BARK AT NIGHT

LEWIS

GRIZZARD

CHILI DAWGS ALWAYS BARK AT NIGHT

VILLARD BOOKS NEW YORK 1989

Some of the material in this book first appeared in the *Atlanta
Journal-Constitution* and is reproduced by permission.

Library of Congress Cataloging-in-Publication Data
Grizzard, Lewis.
Chili dawgs always bark at night / by Lewis Grizzard.
p. cm.
ISBN 0-394-57807-4
  I. Title.
  PN6162.G76   1989
814' .54—dc20   89-40291

Manufactured in the United States of America
9 8 7 6 5 4 3 2
First Edition

FOR CHRISTEL,
who helps a lot

Contents

1 A KINDER, GENTLER NATION

Making America a Kinder, Gentler Nation, 3 · Call It a Conundrum, 5 · America's Newest Killer, 7 · When "The Boys" Grew Up, 9 · Let's Get the Trains on Track, 11 · Why Not a Jerk Patrol?, 13 · On Water Patrol, 15

2 FASHION TIPS

Dress Codes that Need Decoding, 21 · Pulling the Wool Over My Eyes, 23 · Your Guide to Men's Leisure Fashion, 25 · Living the Battle of the Bulge, 27

3 DINING OUT

Fit to Be Tied at the Plaza, 33 · My Dogged Addiction, 35 · Breakfast with a Kick, 37 · Who Needs Self-service?, 38 · The One and Only Vidalia Onion, 41 · Knowing Where to Draw the Line on Carp, 43 · Getting Rid of Ants Is No Picnic, 45 · A Grain of Truth in Straight Talk About Cereal, 47

4 RELIGION

We're All Still in God's Waiting Room, 51 · Giving the Bird to a Turkey, 53 · Humor out of This World, 55 · Pay as You Inter, 57 · Enough Is Enough, 59 · Was It the Lord's Work?, 61

5 THE NEWS

Where No News Is Good News, 67 · Journalism Gone Bonkers, 69 · Call Me "MAODWMNSPCG14HGWS", 71

6 TEE TIME

Why I Get Teed Off, 75 · My Handicap: Women Golfers, 77 · Roughly Speaking, I Play Golf, 79 · "The Snake Rule" of Golf, 80 · The Course of True Golf, 82

7 MAN'S BEST FRIEND

My Dog, the Genius, 87 · Going Nuts Over Squirrels, 89 · The Stranger and the Lost German Shepherd, 91 · My Dog, the Star, 93 · Leading a Dog's Life, 95 · A Deuce No Longer Wild, 97 · Barking Up the Wrong Tree, 99

8 THEY CALL HIM BUBBA

His Name Is Nobody's Business, 103 · The "Bubba" Stereotype, 105

9 THE TROUBLE WITH TEENAGERS

Suggested Courses for Today's Teenager, 109 · Why Teachers Play Hooky, 111 · Recalling My School Daze, 113 · It's Only Sheepskin Deep, 115 · Today's Teenage "Slanguage", 117 · Capital Punishment, 119 · Attention, All You Racist, Sexist Swine, 121 · Is School Lunch Fare Fair?, 123 · Today's Teens Discover a New Hangout, 125

10 ON THE ROAD

Caught Short in Bermuda, 131 · Back to Paradise, 133 · Into the Woods—to Go Camping, 135 · Cabin Fever at 21 Below, 137 · In Lieu of That Swimsuit Issue, 139 · Back-Home Thoughts, 141

11 SPORTS

Ol' Granny's Curse, 147 · My Most Valuable Players, 149 · Casanova Couldn't Get to First Base, 151 · Why I Hate the Yankees, 153 · Little Eddie, R.I.P., 155 · Bike Riders, Beware, 157 · For Sale: One Complete Ski Outfit, 158

12 INTERNATIONAL RELATIONS

Why Not Toss a Coin?, 163 · The Wall Around the Russians, 165 · The Russians Out in the Code, 167 · Sex in Moscow, 169 · In the Huddle with George Bush, 171 · How 'Bout Them Japanese!, 173 · Have You Heard of Boise, Idaho?, 175 · They're Buying American—Literally, 177 · The Rising Sum Will Cost Us, 179

13 WEIGHTY MATTERS

Putting Their Best Chins Forward, 183 · Where Do All Those Lost Pounds Go?, 185 · Cordie Mae's Gain-Weight Diet, 187

14 BAD HABITS

Hints for Sobriety, 193 · Would You Walk a Mile for One?, 195 · How I Quit Smoking, 197 · Going Up in Smoke, 199 · Six Steps to Stop Smoking, Butt Don't Stumble, 201

15 OF TIME AND BIRTH

Children Are Forever, 207 · Memories of My Father, 209 · Of Time and Birth, 211

16 GETTING OLDER

Life Calls No Time-Outs, 217 · Now Ear This, 219 · Roy Orbison's Legacy, 221 · Cheers for a Real-Life Bar,

222 · When I Danced on the Ceiling, 224 · I'm Not Dying to Pay for My Funeral, 226

17 LIFE IN THE TWENTIETH CENTURY

How Times Have Changed, 231 · Fighting Tooth and Nail, 233 · Special Delivery, Posthaste, 235 · Mebbe the Front Porch Should Come Back, 237 · How to Be a Clock-Eyed Manager, 239 · Gone With the Wind, 241 · Horses Drive Me Buggy, 243 · How to Treat a Lady, 245 · Thingamabobs and Whatchamacallits, 247 · Life in the Year 2000, 240

Introduction

Those of you who are reading this book and are not from the South (Georgia in particular) may be somewhat confused by the spelling of one of the words in the title.

That word would be "Dawgs." I know the correct spelling for that word is "D-o-g-s," but in Georgia, where I was born and where I currently live, we don't spell it that way.

We spell it "D-a-w-g-s" because that's the way we pronounce it, and we pronounce it a lot because the University of Georgia, where I went to school and where my heart remains, has had excellent football teams over the past quarter-century and we refer to those teams as the "Dawgs."

Georgia's official nickname is the "Bulldogs," but nobody says that. What people say is "Dawgs," as in "How 'bout them Dawgs!," which also contains some grammatical indiscretions, but it's an honored phrase by Georgia graduates, who use it after victorious games as a means of implying, "My, but isn't our team a glorious group of scholar-athletes who have just kicked (hopefully, Auburn's or Georgia Tech's) butts!"

Georgia also once had a coach named "Butts." Wally Butts, who guided the team in the forties and fifties. As a matter of fact, somebody wrote a book about him and entitled it *No Ifs, No Ands, and a Lot of Butts,* which should indicate the University of Georgia turns out some top book-titling talent as well as football players.

One of the questions readers ask me a great deal is, "Lewis, where do you get the titles for your books?"

I think that's a good question, since my books do not have normal titles like other books have.

I like long titles. My first book was *Kathy Sue Loudermilk, I Love You,* written sometime around the end of World War I. I chose that title in honor of a girl in my school, Kathy Sue Loudermilk, who had large breasts in the fourth grade—by the time she graduated from high school, they had retired her pink sweater.

Then I got musical with *Won't You Come Home, Billy Bob Bailey?,* which was a reference to my crack correspondent Billy Bob Bailey of Ft. Deposit, Alabama, whose dog Rooster once bit Alabama Governor George Wallace at a barbecue/fundraiser in Sylacage, Alabama. Rooster was sick for a week.

Then, another musical allusion, *Don't Sit Under the Grits Tree with Anyone Else but Me.* That book included a piece on how I had sold grits trees to Yankees for great profit.

The others:

- *They Tore Out My Heart and Stomped That Sucker Flat:* again from a piece of music, the brilliant country legend "She Tore Out My Heart and Stomped That Sucker Flat."
- *If Love Were Oil, I'd Be About a Quart Low:* My stepbrother, Ludlow Porch, himself an accomplished author *(It's Not So Neat to See Your Feet)* gave me that one and charged me only fifty dollars for it.
- *Elvis Is Dead and I Don't Feel So Good Myself:* from Mark Twain's line "All great men are dying and I don't feel so good myself."
- *Shoot Low, Boys—They're Ridin' Shetland Ponies.* I was sitting with a friend of mine, Ronnie Jenkins, at Lucille's, a beer joint in Grantville, Georgia. Ronnie and I were both eighteen, but Lucille didn't care how old you were.

As long as you had thirty-five cents, she'd serve you a can of Pabst Blue Ribbon beer.

Ronnie and I had had several Pabst Blue Ribbon beers, and he suddenly said, "Shoot low, boys, they're ridin' Shetland ponies."

I never did know why Ronnie suddenly said that, but it caught me as hilarious and I said to him, "One day, I'm going to write a book and name it what you just said."

After the book was published, several people said the correct phrase is actually "Shoot low, Sheriff, they're ridin' Shetlands," and it is from an old western movie. I don't know if that is true or not, and I don't care. The book sold a lot of copies, and I bought some great stuff with the royalties.

- *My Daddy Was a Pistol and I'm a Son of a Gun:* That's from a Roger Miller song, "Dang Me." I think the publisher had to pay somebody in order to use that title.
- *When My Love Returns from the Ladies Room, Will I Be Too Old to Care?:* I made that up by myself one night at Creekside Cafe in Atlanta, when I checked my watch and determined my date had been in the rest room for nearly half an hour. What do they do in there?
- *Don't Bend Over in the Garden, Granny, You Know Them Taters Got Eyes.* A singer friend of mine, Pat Horine, said that one night when we were laughing about song titles such as, "My Wife Just Ran Off with My Best Friend, and I Miss Him" and "You're the Reason Our Children Are Ugly."

As far as *Chili Dawgs Always Bark at Night* is concerned, I made that one up by myself, too. It came to me at four in the morning after I had eaten three chili dogs from Atlanta's world-famous Varsity Drive-In restaurant, where they serve the best chili dawgs on earth. The Varsity's secret, I think, is that their buns are always fresh and soft and they mix mustard into their chili.

What I was doing up at four in the morning after eating the three Varsity chili dawgs was looking for my jar of Maalox.

A little about the new book:

This is going to be an easy book for you to read because it is a collection of my works and there is no plot, so you don't have to start at the front and work your way to the back if you don't want to.

You can start at the back and work forward, or you can simply open the book in the middle and go whichever way it suits you to go.

You don't have to fold down the ear of one of the pages to keep up with your place while you're reading my book, either, because it really doesn't matter where your place is.

This would be a good book to put into your guest bathroom. I figure the average person can read somewhere between three to four pieces out of this book while he or she is sitting on the john in your guest bathroom. That is, unless he or she has been eating Varsity chili dawgs, which would provide the guest the time and opportunity to read perhaps an entire chapter, or two, depending on whether or not the guest also had onions.

Here are some other titles I suggested for this book that my editor turned down:

- *The Adventures of Johnny Condomseed*
- *Hold Her, Newt, She's Headin' for the Briar Patch*
- *Satanic Nurses*
- *Tammy Faye Bakker Is Uglier than a Bowling Shoe*
- *Chili Dawgs Always Make Me Vomit*

I have an excellent editor, his name is Peter, and maybe if I mention his name in this introduction, he'll offer me a fat new contract for my next book, which may or may not be a novel entitled *Good God, Harvey! They've Stolen Your Ass!*

Yeah, I do write books because you get money for it. Otherwise, I wouldn't do it. Instead, I would get myself a job in a convenience store in Florida and steal lottery tickets.

As many of you know, however, I donated a great deal of the money I have made from writing books toward my little brother Joey's operation.

I can now report that Joey had his operation. A sex-change operation. He is now Joanne, and he is a cocktail waitress and plays golf from the ladies' tees.

I have two reasons for wanting this book to be successful.

One is, I want to buy a pair of white Gucci loafers. I've never owned a pair of white Gucci loafers, and I don't know anybody else who has. I think a pair of white Gucci loafers would look great on me after a game of golf as I sipped a cocktail in the Men's Grill at my golf club or at a Julio Iglesias concert.

(I once got kicked out of an Iglesias concert at the Fox Theatre in Atlanta for singing along with him on "To All the Girls I've Loved Before." If I'd been wearing white Gucci loafers, they probably would have figured I was the Italian version of Willie Nelson and allowed me to stay at the concert.)

I also hope the success of this book might awaken the Pulitzer Prize committee to the fact I've been writing a newspaper column for twelve long years and I still don't have my Pulitzer.

It's not the money I want from a Pulitzer Prize. You don't get much more than a thousand. It's the pride and the prestige involved, and the fact that if I win a Pulitzer, even when my syndicate calls and says, "Your columns have been a little stale lately," they'll have to say, "Your *Pulitzer Prize–winning* columns have been a little stale lately."

I don't know why I can't win a Pulitzer, too. I try just as hard as the next columnist, and during my career I have broken much new ground, what with my exposés of salad bars (they put these little tomatoes way in the back where you can't reach them so they don't have to buy any new little tomatoes), buttermilk (It comes from cows that eat dirt. That's why it tastes so bad), Muammar Qaddafi (he's the same person as baseball pitcher Jacquin Andujar), the Greyhound Bus Company (they pay people to sit next to you and cough), oxygen masks that are supposed to fall down over your seat in airplanes in the unlikely event of cabin depressurization (they don't actually exist), Meryl Streep (she's ugly and I don't care how good she can act), buttered popcorn at movie theaters (It's a ripoff. The only popcorn that gets any butter on it is right at the top), the fact that *The Accidental Tourist* was an awful movie (William Hurt played a piece of Velveeta cheese), members of the National Rifle Association (if they can't find anything else to shoot, they shoot their trucks), and I was the first person to interview God. He said to tell Jimmy Swaggart he was fired.

I'm not certain how many more years I can keep up the grind of four columns per week. I'm almost out of typewriter ribbons, and I lost Detroit because they hired a new woman editor who canceled my column because she said I was a sexist. The dumb broad probably doesn't shave her legs.

So, I want my Pulitzer and I want it as soon as possible. And I want you to enjoy this book. And if you have read this far, go on up to the counter and pay for it. The guy at the Gucci store said if I could get up the down payment for my white loafers, he'd finance the rest of it.

1

A KINDER, GENTLER NATION

Making America a Kinder, Gentler Nation

George Bush has asked for a kinder, gentler America, and I want to do my part in 1989.

Understand that I am usually a kind and gentle person. I am kind to animals, except cats, and I am gentle when it comes to children, unless they are screaming in the seat behind me on an airplane.

But I must admit there are things that cause me not to be kind and gentle, and these are the things I want to learn to accept and be kinder and more gentle about in 1989.

Let us start at the beginning:

Cats: The thing about cats is, they are not to be trusted. A friend of mine's cat snuck behind me once and jumped on my head, causing me to spill the coffee I was drinking. It went all over my lap (the coffee). The cat stayed on my head and danced the merengue.

I did not handle the situation with kindness or gentility. I reached up and removed the cat from my scalp and bit one of its ears off.

Ever tasted a cat ear? They're terrible. But I'm a new man now. If a cat jumps on my head in 1989, I'm not going to bite its ear off. I'm going to poison it, but with a quick-acting potion so it won't suffer for long.

Screaming children in airplanes: I'm not going to ask the flight attendant, "May I have a napkin so I can gag the screaming child?" I'm going to buy the kid a drink. Maybe it will go to sleep.

People affiliated with certain religious organizations who ring my doorbell at an inappropriate time in order to save my soul: Normally, I take out my Uzi machine gun and attempt to blow these people away. From now on, I'll fire a few warning shots before I attempt to blow these people away.

People who drive eight miles an hour in the passing lane on interstate highways: I hate people who do that. They should be arrested and flogged. But that's the old me, not the kinder, gentler me.

From now on, I'm not going to get behind such people and pretend I've got machine guns behind my headlights and fire until the cars erupt in flames.

I'm simply going to take down their tag numbers and find out who they are, where they live, and then I'm going to their houses and bite their cats' ears off.

People who cheat in the twelve-items-or-less express lane in supermarkets: Previously, I have dog-cussed these people and put curses on them like, "May your children grow up to be liberal Democrats."

I'm not going to be that mean-spirited anymore. What I'm going to do is go to the vegetable bin, grab a large cucumber, and beat them about the head and shoulders with it.

Telephones: Telephones never work for me. I either can't get a dial tone, or I get one of those awful noises that sounds like a cat who's just had its ear bitten off, and I slam the receiver down and throw the telephone against the wall.

Not anymore. All I'm going to do now is throw a rock at the television every time I see Cliff Robertson.

Liberal Democrats: I have no use for these people, and when I've run across one at a cocktail party, I've said things like, "Well, how many vicious criminals did Michael Dukakis furlough today?"

But in the immortal words of Dan Quayle, "That was uncalled for."

From now on, I'm going to sneak up behind them and jump on their heads. I'd bite off one of their ears, but it might make me sick.

Call It a Conundrum

Somebody broke into the birth-control clinic at Grady Hospital in Atlanta recently and stole sixteen thousand condoms. I swore I wouldn't write about the incident.

At the time, it seemed too easy. All I would have to do is sit down in front of my typewriter and come up with a few cute lines about condoms, and I'd have a quick "no-brainer" and I could take the rest of the day off.

Anybody could write about the theft of sixteen thousand condoms, couldn't they? Sure they could. But let them try to make up something funny about Yassir Arafat not being allowed to speak at the United Nations or animal rights.

But then I began to act and think sensibly. Somebody steals sixteen thousand condoms only once in a columnist's career. I decided I couldn't pass up the opportunity.

In fact, I'm not sure this wasn't the first condom heist in history, and even if it wasn't the first, it certainly had to be the biggest.

Several questions concerning the theft began to creep into my mind.

Like, how much do sixteen thousand condoms weigh?

Would they weigh so much or be so unwieldy to handle that the job involved more than one person?

What went through the robber's (or robbers') mind when he or she came upon the sixteen thousand condoms?

Did the thief think, "Hey, there's sixteen thousand condoms here. Let's see, if I could sell them for fifty cents each, I'd make eight thousand dollars."

Or did the thief think, "Just for kicks, I'll take these sixteen thousand condoms with me and see if anybody writes about it?"

Or was the thought, "I think I'll stage a huge group sex party. I'll need these condoms, of course, and then I'll invite Audrey and Henry and Rebecca and Grover and Peggy and Ralph, etc."?

If it was the thief's idea to throw such a party, I'd like to be invited—if not to engage in the activities to at least study and take notes and later chronicle the event for history. Maybe the Romans held orgies that required sixteen thousand condoms, but I don't think it's been done recently.

Some more questions came up.

If somebody steals sixteen thousand condoms, where do they hide them? Could you get sixteen thousand condoms in a closet? In the garage?

A locker at the bus station certainly wouldn't hold all of them. What if you buried them?

If the thief did bury the sixteen thousand condoms, would he or she take a friend out to the burial site and say, "Guess what I've got buried under here?"

The friend might respond, "A Brink's truck filled with money."

"No," the thief would explain, "anybody could steal a Brink's truck filled with money. I've got sixteen thousand condoms buried under here."

There's one other thought I had. Perhaps the condom thief was acting as a humanitarian. Perhaps he or she took the sixteen thousand condoms and plans to distribute them around the United States as a means of helping put a stop to unwanted pregnancies and the spread of sexually transmitted diseases.

We always think the worst of people when we should think the best of them.

Imagine this person handing out condoms across the width and breath of our great nation as a favor to his or her fellow citizens.

Johnny Condomseed. It might be. It just might be.

America's Newest Killer

Maybe all of us should band together and say "Enough is enough. Please don't tell us what else will kill us."

Where is all this going to end? First it was cigarettes. We are still being warned cigarettes will cause lung cancer or emphysema, not to mention turn our fingers and teeth yellow.

A lot of Americans have quit smoking. They want the ones who haven't to do so immediately. Nonsmokers and smokers, I predict, will have a civil war eventually and kill off great numbers of both sides all in the name of health.

And cholesterol. Eat stuff that really tastes good and cholesterol will clog your arteries, and one day you'll be sitting there eating a couple of fried eggs and you'll drop dead of a heart attack.

"He should have watched his diet," they'll say at your funeral.

You can get cancer from just about everything, it seems. We mentioned smoking. But there's asbestos, eating smoked foods, or drinking too much coffee.

And speaking of drinking, go right ahead and have another scotch, but you know your liver is rotting with every sip.

Then there's AIDS. I don't want to talk about AIDS anymore.

And let's don't forget how many near misses there are in commercial aviation. You're sitting there in 23A and suddenly there's a 727 coming down the aisle.

Also, we can't forget that the ozone layer is disappearing from our atmosphere and one day we'll all be fried because there won't be anything left to protect us from the sun.

So, let's say none of that gets you. Great, except now there's something new to worry about—RADON!

You quit smoking, drinking, and eating fatty foods. You exercise every day, brush regularly with tartar-control toothpaste, and have annual checkups from your doctor.

You've eaten cereal until it's coming out of your ears, you take all sorts of vitamins—and speaking of cereal, you even eat yours with prunes on top.

You're the best friend your colon ever had.

But you're still not safe because radon is here and it's coming after you.

It's down there in the ground under your house. You can't see radon, and you can't smell it, but it's there.

It sneaks up through your basement. It comes up pipes and through cracks and you breathe it, and you might as well have kept sucking on those cigarettes, because radon can give you lung cancer, too.

If you want to be safe from this newest killer, you've got to buy a gadget that measures radon in your house, and if you've got it, then you have to get some guy to come over and make an assortment of repairs, and that's going to cost you.

Wouldn't we be better off if nobody told us about things like radon? Sure it might pick a few of us off, but we wouldn't have to lie in our beds at night wondering how much radon the uranium under our condos is producing—and was that noise you just heard downstairs the Radon Monster coming to get you?

Worry kills, too. Would somebody please mention that to the Surgeon General.

When "The Boys" Grew Up

"The weekly meeting of the Slim Pickens Chapter of the Beer-Swilling, Tobacco-Chewing, Possum-Eating, Card-Playing Brotherhood of America will please come to order," announced Shorty Milsaps, club president.

The boys gunned down the last swallows of their beer and gave Shorty their attention.

"Men," Shorty began, "I must bring before the brotherhood tonight a serious matter that could affect this organization as nothing before ever has.

"As you might have heard, the Supreme Court has ruled that private clubs may no longer discriminate in accepting members.

"I'm here tonight to tell you that the time may come when we might have to accept women into this brotherhood."

A hush fell over the startled listeners.

"You serious, Shorty?" asked Cootie Carnes.

"As your mother-in-law's drawers, Cootie," replied Shorty.

There was much murmuring and cursing, and finally Gilbert Harskins said, "This is the last place we got, men.

"You can't get away from women at work no more. They on television giving the news and they're all over the golf course and they've even got in the Rotary Club.

"I wouldn't be surprised to see one playin' outfield for the Pirates before it's over."

"Hell," said Marvin Coddlemeyer, "if we get women in here, we going to have to change a lot of things."

"Like what?" asked Gilbert Harskins.

"Well, for one thing, we won't be able to spit on the floor or have the weekly belching contest. Women don't go in for spittin' on the floor or belching.

"We'll also have to quit telling nasty jokes, and Leon Caldwell won't be able to do that funny thing where he paints eyes on his belly and uses his navel for a mouth and pantomimes 'She Was Just a Stableman's Daughter, but All the Horsemen Knew Her.' "

"That'd be a shame," said Cootie Carnes.

"I'll tell you what else," said Marvin Coddlemeyer.

"Women will want to have congealed salad and celery sticks instead of possum and sweet potatoes, and I guarantee you it won't be a month before they'll be sittin' around here drinkin' white wine and talking about their hairstylists."

"Marvin's right," said Cootie Carnes. "A man's just got to have a place he can go now and then and just be himself and say what he wants to and scratch where it itches. Dammit, Leon, quit spittin' on my shoes."

Curtis Knowles hadn't said a word during the entire discussion. Curtis had been married four times, once to a lady lawyer, and was held as an expert on females.

"Boys," he said, "if a woman can sit here with us and listen to all the bull and put up with chewin', spittin', belchin', cussin', and Leon Caldwell's navel, I say she's what I've been lookin' for all my life and hadn't been able to find. A woman who would put up with a man just bein' himself."

A hush fell over the crowd.

"I move we put an ad in the paper," said Cootie Carnes. "I'd like to meet a woman like that myself."

Let's Get the Trains on Track

I've heard enough about airlines taking care of their planes so that they break in half on landing or the top rips off in flight.

I don't want to know anymore about how many near-miss midair collisions there are and about how we don't have enough air-traffic controllers.

And I don't want to hear anything else about unhappy airline employees. Deliver me from the guy who's mad at his boss and is in charge of making certain all the bolts are tight for the flight to Omaha.

I've been saying this for years and nobody will listen to me, but maybe now, with all the frightening things that are going on in the airline industry, somebody will.

Bring back the train!

All we've got now in this country as a passenger rail system is the government-subsidized Amtrak that is far behind the systems of other countries. So much so, it is an embarrassment.

The French and the Germans and the Japanese know something about passenger trains. They run them at speeds over two hundred miles per hour and very few of them ever get hijacked, rerouted during bad weather, or canceled because there's nobody to drive them.

We need an alternative to air travel. Driving is unsafe and tiresome, and if you want to ride the bus, you'll get a seat next to some guy with a bad cough and there's nowhere to go to get away from him.

But a train. If the French can build one that runs smoothly at two hundred miles an hour, certainly we can.

Let's say you are traveling from Chicago to Atlanta. That's about seven hundred miles.

To fly, you have to get to O'Hare from the Loop, which is a pain and costs you. You leave at 4:00 P.M. for a 5:30 flight.

Your plane backs out of the gate at 5:45 and doesn't actually take off until 6:15. The flight is just over an hour, but due to heavy traffic at Atlanta's Hartsfield, you have to hold for twenty minutes.

You finally touch down in Atlanta three hours and change after you left for O'Hare.

But then you've got to ride the shuttle to the main terminal and wait on your bags. After that, it's a cab ride into town. You get to your hotel after what has at least been a four-hour ordeal.

But the two hundred-mile-an-hour train from Chicago to Atlanta:

It leaves Union Station, a short cab ride from the Loop, where you work. Zoom, off you go. It's smooth. It's relaxing. There's a guy next to you coughing, so you go to the club car for a drink.

There's a few quick stops, like the old days when the train stopped at every crossing. Maybe there's ten minutes in Louisville. And another in Nashville. And Chattanooga.

You arrive in Atlanta's downtown station, let's say in five hours.

It's about the same as the flight, only think of the hassle

you've avoided and the money you've saved in ground transportation.

Putting a modern, efficient passenger system to work in this country would probably cost trillions, I admit.

So let's make peace with the Russians and then use all the money we're spending on missiles to bring back the trains.

What a great idea, and I know how to get the president to agree.

Take Air Force One away from him and put him out there in the crowded, unfriendly skies with the rest of us.

Why Not a Jerk Patrol?

New York City has formed what I presume to be the first bigot patrol in the long history of law enforcement in this country.

The move, announced last week, was instigated after outbreaks of racial violence in the city, "just like down South," as Mayor Ed Koch put it.

Before racial incidents occurred in such places as New York's Howard Beach, Mayor Koch thought bias and prejudice ended just south of Baltimore someplace.

According to reports I read, New York's bigot patrol will work like this:

Cops in plainclothes or disguise will go into neighborhoods with a history of racial disturbances and act as bait for bigots or, bigot-bait, whichever you prefer.

Black decoys will work Howard Beach, for instance, to deal with anyone manifesting racist tendencies.

Assistant Chief John Holmes, commander of the new unit, explained it all this way:

"We want to say to bigots: the next time you set upon somebody in the streets, he is liable to be a police officer and you are liable to be under arrest."

I hope Archie Bunker has heard about all this.

But why not a bigot patrol? We tried legislation and education as a means of ending prejudice and that hasn't worked. Perhaps a little police muscle will do the trick.

And if the bigot patrol is successful, think of the other social misfits we could round up and haul off in a paddy wagon.

For example, we could have an ugly patrol.

"I'm sorry, sir, but you'll have to come with me downtown."

"But what's the charge, Officer?"

"You're in violation of the city's ugly ordinance. Nobody with a big nose, ears that poke out, or, in your case, is cross-eyed, can be on the streets before dark."

I'd like to see a cliché patrol, too. If there's anything I can't stand it's people who use clichés.

Anybody who says, "Have a nice one," "Hot enough for you?," "So how's the wife?," or "You know" more than five times in any sentence could cool their heels in the slammer for a few days.

I'd get people off the streets whose clothes don't match, too.

"Spread 'em, Sucker," a member of the *GQ* patrol might say, "that tie does not go with that jacket you're wearing. It's vermin like you that give civilization a bad name."

Maybe we could also have a jerk patrol. Think how much better life would be if we didn't have to put up with people who do jerky, annoying things like drive forty in the passing lane, talk loudly in a movie theater, or throw their gum on the sidewalk for some innocent, law-abiding citizen to step on.

People who sneeze as they sit on the stool next to you while you're eating a bowl of soup in a diner, who bring large cassette players onto public conveyances and play music to have a nervous breakdown by, who play slowly on a golf course, who get into the express lane at grocery stores with more than twelve items, who don't put their hand over their heart when the national anthem is being played, who don't use deodorant, have a bad case of dandruff and idiotic ideas you don't agree with.

I don't know why somebody didn't think of using the police to get rid of all our social warts and blemishes before. It's worked in other countries—so why not here?

As Mayor Koch says, "Up against the wall, you redneck mother."

On Water Patrol

They were talking about those poor souls in Wheeling, West Virginia, on the news.

Residents are being urged to conserve water, the announcer said, and not to take baths or showers. P.U.

There was that million-gallon diesel oil spill that got into the Ohio River and eventually oozed its way down to Wheeling, cutting off the city's water supply.

Most of us have never been in a shortage-of-water situation, and we figure we never will.

Turn on the faucet, there's water. There always has been, there always will be.

But I have a different viewpoint.

I grew up in a family where water conservation was a way

of life. I still cringe when I see pictures of Niagara Falls. The whole thing looks to me like somebody is wasting a lot of good water.

My family got its water from a well. I don't know much about wells, but ours was a Corvair.

"We're going to have to be careful with water," my mother must have said a million times, "the well's low."

I always knew ahead of time when the well was getting low. When you turned on a faucet, a hissing, blowing, belching sound would emerge, followed by two or three drops of water of a distinct brown hue.

Here are my family's water-conserving rules:

1. Never leave a faucet dripping. The penalty for failing to adhere to the first rule: My mother would yell at you, "How many times have I told you not to leave a faucet dripping? If you had lived through the Depression like I did, you would understand these things."

2. Use the absolute minimum amount of water for your bath. My mother, on constant water patrol, would burst unannounced into the bathroom, and if the water in our tub covered your little toe, she would launch into a lecture on gas rationing during World War II.

3. Never flush the toilet more than once per use. My mother was so strict on this one, I still get a thrill out of staying in a hotel room where I can flush the toilet as many times as I please.

As a matter of fact, I have more respect and appreciation for water than anybody else I know. My background obviously is the reason for this.

Nothing makes my day like a shower with strong water pressure. A shower with a mere trickle makes me consider joining a terrorist group.

I love a cold glass of ice water the first thing in the morning. It puts out any fires still smoldering from the night before.

I love rinsing off my face with warm water after shaving. The skin tingles, the eyes open, bring on the world.

If it weren't for water, I couldn't make coffee in the morning, and scotch drinkers would be even more obnoxious than they already are.

If it weren't for water, Seve Ballesteros, a foreigner, would have won the Masters golf tournament a few years ago, keeping Jack Nicklaus from his heroic and nostalgic victory.

All I'm trying to say is, we occasionally should consider just how precious water is. Wheeling, West Virginia, now knows.

Nothing like a citywide outbreak of B.O. to drive that point home.

2

FASHION TIPS

Dress Codes that Need Decoding

While actress Whoopi Goldberg was in Atlanta recently for her one-woman show, she stayed at the downtown Ritz Carlton Hotel.

She was refused entrance to the Ritz restaurant, however, because she didn't look like the Ritz thinks you ought to look when you eat in one of their hotels.

Let's just say that Whoopi will never make the cover of *Mademoiselle.*

I often have wondered why restaurants and bars are so picky about how somebody looks or dresses when they come in and offer their business.

Take the sign that says NO SHIRT, NO SHOES, NO SERVICE.

Does this mean as long as I have on a shirt and shoes I can take off my pants and still get the bacon cheeseburger?

The least they could do in a restaurant with a sign like that is to say, "You can't come in without your shirt or shoes, but I'll take your order if you'll just wait outside while it's cooking."

I've never been fond of the sign that says GENTLEMEN ARE REQUIRED TO WEAR JACKETS AND TIES.

I've always figured restaurants have rules like that to make certain they don't get any riffraff.

But some very riffraffy people wear ties. Ed Meese. Jimmy Swaggart. Al Capone wore ties, didn't he?

I don't know if medical science has looked into it, but I would suppose that wearing a jacket and tie and trying to eat in a place where they won't allow you to drink your beer from a bottle would not be that good for the digestion.

The jacket restricts movement and the tie probably is some detriment to circulation. This dress code, then, could lead to such maladies as heartburn, indigestion, and even ulcers.

If it turns out such restaurants have a deal going with the Maalox people, I wouldn't be surprised.

I saw a sign in a hotel bar in Jacksonville, Florida, recently that completely baffled me.

It said CASUAL, STYLISH ATTIRE ONLY.

The first thing I did when I saw that sign was to look and see what I was wearing. I was wearing a golf shirt, khaki slacks, and loafers with no socks.

There was no question that I was casual, but was I stylish as well?

It depended, I suppose, on various personal points of view.

"Something out of a 1956 Sears catalog," detractors might say. "Definitely not stylish."

A more mature person might say, however, "Middle-aged preppy, huh? Very stylish, please come in."

With some trepidation, I walked into the place and took a seat at the bar.

"Before I order," I said to the bartender, a woman, "do you think my outfit is stylish enough to be in here?"

"You'll do," she said. "Now, what ya drankin'?"

Whoopi! I ordered a beer in a bottle.

Pulling the Wool
Over My Eyes

I found my old high school letter jacket the other day. I was looking for something else in the back of a closet at my mother's house and came upon it—blue with off-white leather sleeves and a block *N* sewn on the front.

I had forgotten it even existed. I suppose that twenty-four years ago when I graduated from high school, I simply cast it aside as I leaped into the more material collegiate world.

"I put it up for you and kept it," my mother said, "in case you ever wanted it again."

I played basketball and baseball at Newnan High School. I lettered in both sports, which is how I got the jacket in the first place. My number, 12, is stitched on one of the sleeves. The face of a tiger—our mascot—is on the other.

Enough years have passed now that I probably could lie about my high school athletic career and get away with most of it.

I know guys who barely made the varsity who've managed to move up to all-state status with the passing of enough years.

But I'll be honest. I was an average athlete, if that. I averaged maybe ten points a game in basketball, and shot the thing on every opportunity that came to me.

"Grizzard is the only person who never had a single assist in his entire basketball career," an ex-teammate was telling someone in my presence. "That's because he never passed the ball."

I hit over .300 my senior year in baseball, but they were all bloop singles except for one of those bloopers that rolled in some high weeds in right field. By the time the ball was found, I was around the bases for the winning run.

"Why don't you take it home with you?" my mother suggested after I had pulled the jacket out of the closet. "Maybe you'll have some children one day and they might like to see it."

I reminded my mother I was forty-one and down three marriages, and the future didn't look that bright for offspring. But I suppose a mother can dream.

I did bring the jacket home with me. Alone, up in my bedroom, in front of a mirror, I pulled it over me for the first time in a long time.

A lot of names came back with the jacket. Clay, John, Buddy, Russell, Richard, Al. And Dudley and the Hound, who's still looking for his first base hit since he was fifteen.

And then there was Wingo, of course, the best high school shortstop I ever saw until a ground ball hit a pebble one day and bounced up and broke his jaw.

Ever hear that haunting song "Where Are the Men I Used to Sport With?"

They've all got kids, I guess, and their mothers are happy.

It's funny about my jacket. It still fit well on my arms and shoulders, but I couldn't get it to button anymore.

I guess some shrinkage can be expected after all those years of neglect in the closet.

Your Guide to Men's Leisure Fashion

My interest and expertise in the area of men's fashion are well documented. I, for instance, predicted the coming of the leisure suit back in the late sixties.

What led me to such a projection was the sudden falloff in the purchase of Nehru jackets, not to mention the fact a group of geologists digging in the mountains of West Virginia discovered the world's richest vein of polyester.

I also forecast the fall of the leisure suit. This was after four conventioneers perished in their Las Vegas hotel when one dropped a cigar ash on the pants of his leisure suit.

He was engulfed in flames in a matter of seconds. His three companions succumbed to the dense acrid fumes from their friend's lime-green leisure suit.

Once, while I was temporarily stationed in sunny Florida covering warm weather for the rest of the country, where it was cold and dismal, I was hanging out at the pool at my hotel, working on my tan, when I noticed other male visitors were suffering from various levels of warm-weather fashion impairment.

Women, of course, have the annual *Sports Illustrated* swimsuit issue to guide them as to what to wear once spring and summer finally arrive.

Men have nothing to guide them. And it shows.

Fortunately, I am also an expert on menswear at the beach, around the pool, and in the hotel lobby.

What many men here do wrong is wear socks that are the same color as their shorts. This is tacky. This is unforgivable.

A man who wears socks the same color as his shorts is a bowler or builds cabinets in his basement or contributes to television evangelists.

To be absolutely correct, a man should wear no socks whatsoever with a pair of shorts. If a man insists on wearing socks with his shorts, he should at least stick to white.

One other thing a man should consider is never to be guilty of New Jerseyitis. Men suffering from this condition wear sandals with their shorts, not to mention over-the-calf, black stretch hose.

Jesus wore sandals, it is true. But he didn't wear those awful socks with them, and that's why New Jersey—especially Newark—turned out the way it did.

Here are some other don'ts in the area of men's leisure fashion:

- Don't wear a tank top. If you must wear a tank top, at least make certain you have a tattoo to go with it so people will think you've been out to sea since the mid-sixties and don't know any better.
- Don't wear anything that features a picture of a pelican, a pink flamingo, or a beer can.
- Don't wear one of those skimpy European men's bathing suits. If you do, you'll embarrass God, who didn't have skimpy European bathing suits in mind when he created man.
- More on socks. Don't wear tube socks with your shorts or swimsuit. This ain't the Moose Club annual picnic and softball game.
- Don't wear clip-on sunglasses. If you do, it suggests you arrived by bus and once wore leisure suits until the Surgeon General declared them harmful to your health.
- Don't wear white shoes with a matching white belt. That went out with Wildroot Cream Oil for your hair.

- Don't wear a silly hat. If communists went to the beach, they'd wear silly hats.

As for me, I'm off to the pool again in my Ralph Lauren swimsuit ($575), my Calvin Klein terry-cloth robe ($1,500), my Gucci leather pool slippers ($2,750), and my Bill Blass designer sunglasses ($14,000).

I take no fashion risks. Why should you?

Living the Battle of the Bulge

I made a major decision recently. I decided to buy myself a pair of blue jeans.

A forty-one-year-old man should not take on such a thing without first giving it a great deal of thought, which I thought I had done.

First, I asked myself if this was a first sign of middle-aged craziness.

Men do a lot of strange things when afflicted by that condition. They quit their jobs at the bank and go off somewhere to become wood-carvers or fishing guides.

Others leave their wives and buy themselves sports cars, while still others have hair transplants, date girls—girls whose first names end in *i* (Tami, Debbi, Staci), and wear gold neck-chains.

But, I decided, none of that could be happening to me. I'm

not going to quit my job, I have plenty of hair, and I took out Tami, Debbi, and Staci (one at a time) and none worked out. I had underdrawers older than all three.

Second, I had to ask myself if I could still fit into a pair of jeans.

I stopped wearing jeans after I graduated from high school. I was quite thin in high school and my jeans fitted me perfectly.

I am by no means obese now, but I have noticed my body taking on a different and more rounded shape in an area that may be described as the navel and surrounding areas.

It's caused, I thought, by fallen chest arches.

But don't they advertise those jeans with a "skosh more room" for the mature jean-wearer?

I went to the department store and found the menswear department.

"How may I help you?" the salesman asked.

"I'd like a pair of jeans," I replied.

"And what waist size?" said the salesman, eyebrows raised.

"Thirty-four," I answered.

"Let's start at thirty-six and see where it takes us," the salesman suggested.

I couldn't get the zipper up all the way on the 36s.

The 38s fit okay in the back, but they were still a bit too tight in the front and gave me the distinct look of being about three months pregnant.

I even tried on a pair of 40s. I have a rather small backside. There's enough room in the seat of that pair of jeans for a small company of Chinese soldiers to bivouac.

"I'm afraid, sir," said the salesman, "you have the two-bellies."

"The two-bellies?"

"Indeed, sir. What happens to some men who reach middle age, they develop two distinct, shall we say, midsections?

"They have one just above their belly button and then another one below it. The two-bellies makes it almost impossible for one to fit snugly or comfortably in a pair of jeans, even with the extra 'skosh.' "

So I had only been kidding myself when I thought I could still fit into blue jeans.

I'm a two-belly, and my blue-jean days are sadly behind me.

"Could I interest you," the salesman asked, "in a fabric with more give? Say, polyester?"

God, the ravages of age.

3

DINING OUT

Fit to Be Tied
at the Plaza

I was staying at the Plaza Hotel in New York recently (my publisher was paying for the room, that's why I wasn't at a Motel 6 in Newark), and I went to have lunch in one of the hotel's spiffy restaurants.

For the occasion, I wore a blue blazer, accentuated by a pair of khaki trousers and a white golf shirt I'd worn only once before.

I knew I was in trouble the moment I saw the maître d'. He was a tall wisp of a fellow who was probably born with his nose turned up that way.

I wasn't absolutely certain he was light in his loafers, but when he traveled across the restaurant escorting guests to their tables, he touched the floor only once or twice.

"Table for three," I said to the maître d', once he had landed back at his station.

He looked at me as if he were looking at a dead cat in the highway. The right side of his lip curled upward, his nostrils half flared, and the lid of his left eye went to half-mast.

"Gentlemen," he said, "are required to wear ties when they dine here."

There are a number of phrases I enjoy saying at times such as these, but my two companions were ladies, and I was afraid Donald Trump, who owns the Plaza, might be within earshot, so I abstained.

I wear ties only to funerals of close relatives or heads of state. I stopped wearing ties during the late to middle seventies because they made me feel uncomfortable.

I especially hate to eat while wearing a tie. Once I was at a banquet and they served barbecued chicken with lots of red sauce on it.

My tie at the beginning of the meal was blue. At the end, it was red. I gave the tie to my dog. He ate it.

I'm also convinced ties restrict the blood flow to the brain, causing such disorders as forgetfulness, blurred eyesight, and even criminal tendencies.

Al Capone was rarely seen without a tie. The same goes, incidentally, for Richard Nixon.

Anyway, I don't see what difference it makes whether or not you wear a tie into a restaurant at least as long as you are wearing a jacket and clean underwear.

I told the Plaza maître d' I didn't own a tie, and he went into a closet and fetched one.

It was black. Perfect for a blue blazer.

The trouble was, I couldn't remember how to tie a tie. Neither of my companions could either.

Getting terribly hungry now, I asked for help from the lady checking coats. She did a little better than the rest of us. When she finished tying the tie around my neck, the thin part that's supposed to be short was long, and the big part that's supposed to be long was short.

Although I now looked like a complete idiot, wearing an incorrectly tied tie with a golf shirt, I was shown to my table.

I chuckled as I recalled a sign I saw recently in one of Atlanta's Long Horn Steak Houses. Long Horns don't care much about pretension.

The sign said NO SHIRT, NO SHOES, NO SERVICE. BRA AND PANTIES OPTIONAL.

The meal was excellent. I got mayonnaise on my tie.

My Dogged Addiction

If you're addicted to drugs or alcohol, you can go someplace like the Betty Ford Clinic and get help.

But where do you go if you're addicted to chili dogs?

Yes, chili dogs. Those wonderful hot dogs with lots of chili on them and mustard and onions on the chili that the mere mention of which makes my mouth water, my heart rate speed up, and my stomach literally beg to be fed as many of these delights as it can hold.

I had my first chili dog when I was twelve. My father took me to Atlanta's legendary Varsity, the world's largest outdoor drive-in.

My father ordered me a chili dog, I took the first bite of it, and I was hooked.

During my three years in exile in Chicago, I formulated a scheme to get chili dogs from the Varsity delivered to me.

I started dating a girl I met on a trip back home to Atlanta. Every other week I would fly her to Chicago.

"And would you mind," I would ask, "stopping by the Varsity on your way to the airport and bringing me fourteen dozen chili dogs."

Later, it became clearly evident to the young lady that I looked forward to the chili dogs more than I looked forward to seeing her.

"It's me or the chili dogs," she eventually said.

I often wonder what ever happened to her.

I had heart surgery in 1982. The doctors said I could have anything I wanted to eat for my preoperation dinner.

I sent for Varsity chili dogs. Had I died under the knife the next day, at least I would have had a satisfying last meal.

For years I've tried to decide why Varsity chili dogs remain the best I've ever eaten.

The hot dogs are good and so is the chili, but it's the buns that really do it. The Varsity, somebody was telling me, steams its buns. There's nothing better than a steamy bun.

But I must admit my chili dog addiction is becoming a problem.

I can't eat them like I used to and not pay a painful price.

The other night, for instance, I went to the Varsity and had three chili dogs with mustard and raw onions.

I also had an order of french fries and I topped that off with a Varsity fried apple pie with ice cream on it.

I went to bed at eleven. The chili dogs hit at about two.

My stomach felt like I had eaten a large box of nails. It made strange sounds like *goooorp!* and *brriiip!*

I got out of bed, took six Rolaids, two Alka-Seltzers and drank a six-pack of Maalox. Nothing helped.

I'll never eat another chili dog, I said to myself.

Those addicted to any substance often say things like that, but they rarely stick to it.

I know I'll be back at the Varsity soon, woofing down chili dogs. And, later, the agony and the *goooorf*s and *brriiip*s will be back.

My stomach and I simply will have to learn to live with a certain fact.

That is, chili dogs always bark at night.

Breakfast with a Kick

For years I have put up with modern-day nutritionists telling me what I can or cannot put into my stomach.

At one time or other, I've sworn off red meat, eggs, bacon, sugar, and all sorts of other things I enjoy eating. If we listen to health-food advice, all we would be allowed to put in our stomachs would be something animals graze on, bee pollen, and various sorts of bran.

I don't know about anybody else, but eating a diet like that probably would make it necessary to spend a great deal of time in the bathroom, and I've other things to do.

Anyway, I have put up with the nutritionists—as I would any other do-gooders—but now they have gotten personal.

In case you missed it, the Coca-Cola Company is out with a campaign suggesting you drink Coke at breakfast.

They might as well have suggested that along with your Coke you start the day with two Twinkies, a Little Debbie Snack Cake, and a Tootsie Roll. Various nutrition experts expressed shock and dismay (not to be confused with the rock group of the same name) at the thought that Americans might do something so ill-advised as chase down breakfast with a soft drink.

"Breakfast is the most important meal of the day, especially for children," said one so-called food expert. "Coca-Cola should be more responsible and not suggest Americans start their day on a poor nutritional note."

Horsefeathers and grape nuts!

I've been drinking Coke for breakfast for years. In Russia I couldn't find a Coke, so I drank a Pepsi, warm. I'd saved what little ice I could find for the vodka. I'll admit I'm no health specimen, but I don't think I'd be in this good a shape without my Coke in the morning. You know how most of us feel when we get up—groggy and sluggish, ill-tempered, slack-eyed, and loop-legged.

I might start with a cup of coffee, but all that usually does for me is get one of my eyes open and start a fire in a region just behind my navel.

But a Coke. It goes down so smoothly. It puts out the fire. It refreshes—and bring on the day, I think I can make one more. I began drinking Coke for breakfast some twenty years ago when I had a job that demanded I be at work at five-thirty in the morning.

That was when you could still find Coke in those little six-ounce bottles, as the Lord intended.

I would start each day with a couple of those little Cokes, and if anybody had taken them away from me, I would have been a complete failure at my job and my career would have been ruined.

One more thing, as a Southerner, I simply must stand fast against anybody who would want to take Coke, with its roots planted deeply in the South, away from me in the morning. Give them Coke and, perish the thought, grits could be next.

Who Needs Self-service?

Several days ago, I was eating in a fast-food restaurant. Which one isn't that important here, but they have awful chili. It's too runny and there's too many tomatoes.

A couple seated across from me finished their meal. The man got up first and headed for the exit.

The woman said to the man, "Aren't you going to clean off your part of the table?"

The man said in reply, "Certainly not. I'm not an employee here. I just came in for lunch."

I rose to give the man a standing ovation and knocked over my container of chili, which spilled onto the floor.

For years I have stood foursquare against cleaning off my table at fast-food restaurants.

For one thing, it makes me feel like I'm back at the grammar-school cafeteria.

You walk in, get in line, and pick up your tray of food; then you carry your food to your table, eat it, and you're expected to clean your mess.

Every time I go through all that, I can hear Mrs. Bowers, my second-grade teacher, saying, "You can't go out to the playground until you've eaten the rest of your English peas."

But there is a more important issue here. If fast-food restaurants can convince you to clean up after yourself—as is mostly the case—it means they don't have to hire somebody to do it for you.

Think of all the jobs that would be created if all of us customers said to fast-food restaurants, "You want the table cleaned up, then hire somebody to do it."

For instance, McDonald's could put that silly clown to work as a busboy and pay him overtime.

I'm not certain what has happened to service in this country, but there seems to be less of it than ever. Consider:

- The only way you can get food in most airports is to do the cafeteria-line bit and then pay the sullen cashier.
- If you have bags, try carrying them with one hand while juggling food and drink on a tray with the other.

Since the Federal Aviation Administration doesn't provide statistics, there is no telling how many passengers are scalded in airport cafeterias each year by dropping their trays and getting hot coffee in their hair.

- You have to pump your own gasoline most times these days.
- There are no longer ushers in movie houses to show you to an empty seat.
- An ever-increasing number of grocery stores insist you unload your own buggy at the checkout line.
- What's next after a haircut? Is the barber going to insist I sweep the floor?

All this self-service nonsense began with the salad bar. Restaurants discovered people would actually get up and make their own salads.

I've said it once and I'll say it again: I want somebody to bring my salad to me, because when I go out to eat I prefer not lifting a finger.

I also didn't clean my table after eating at the fast-food restaurant the other day, either, and I have made a pact with myself never to do so again.

As for the chili I spilled on the floor, that's where it belonged in the first place.

The One and Only Vidalia Onion

Whenever I am confronted by atheists, I simply make the point that if there weren't a God and He (or She) didn't love us, there wouldn't be such a thing as the beloved Vidalia onion.

Think about it: Vidalia onions, which are sweet and mild, grow only in a small part of southeast Georgia.

Some have tried to duplicate the Vidalia in other parts of the country, but to no avail.

God, I am convinced, was traveling through what was to become southeast Georgia during the six days of creation and said, "Let there be a sweet, mild onion, and let it grow here and here only."

It was just another of the many blessings God gave us, such as spring, cool breezes, the beach, and frequent-flyer points.

I must admit, however, that I have had a problem with Vidalia onions over the years. I usually buy them in great quantities.

I am afraid if I don't, the Arabs will get control of Vidalias and send the price up so far I can't buy them anymore.

My problem is that I can't eat my onions fast enough, and some of my supply turn funny colors and begin to smell.

Because I absolutely abhor throwing out spoiled Vidalia onions, I set about to find a way to keep them fresh for long periods of time.

Finally, I have the answer.

Friends invited me to dinner recently, and delicious baked Vidalia onions were served.

During the meal, I asked, "Do you have a problem keeping your Vidalias fresh?"

"Of course not," the husband answered. "I've got fifty pounds of them stored right now. I'll be eating Vidalia onions all winter. The best way to keep Vidalias," he went on, "is to put them in panty hose."

"Panty hose?"

"Yes," the wife explained. "You take a pair of panty hose and cut off the top part.

"Then you put an onion all the way to the place where your foot goes. Then you tie a knot just above that onion and put in another on top of it. When the panty hose are full of onions, you hang them up somewhere and they stay absolutely fresh.

"What you are doing is keeping the onions from touching one another, which is one reason they go bad if you leave them stored in, say, a sack."

"I hope you don't mind if I tell the rest of the nation about this," I said to my friends.

"Fine, but I don't believe you should mention us by name," said the husband while his wife was not in the room.

"It could be a little embarrassing if you wrote that my wife could get fifty pounds of Vidalia onions in a pair of her panty hose."

I put my hand on what was left of my baked Vidalia and swore I would be discreet.

Knowing Where to Draw the Line on Carp

As far as I know, my late grandfather never read *The New York Times*. He read the Bible, *The Market Bulletin*, and a Sears Rocbuck catalog, but I just can't picture him dealing with the likes of R. W. Apple, Jr., William Safire, and Flora Lewis.

I think he would have been astounded if he had ever picked up a *Times*, as I did the other day, and read a front-page story about how scientists have been fooling around with his most unfavorite fish, the carp.

The *Times* story, displayed at the bottom left of page one opposite a George Bush campaign yawner, explained how scientists have taken a growth gene out of trout and have implanted it in carp, thus making it possible to grow bigger carp.

"Who in the devil," my grandfather would have said, peering over the top of the *Times*, "would want a bigger carp?"

My grandfather was a kind and gentle man, but there were a few things he hated.

Among these were opera singers on *The Ed Sullivan Show*, Jehovah's Witnesses, and carp.

"Sorriest fish there's ever been, the carp," my grandfather would say. "It's too hard to clean and too bony to eat."

On one of our fishing trips to Sibley's Pond, something grabbed my hook and down went my cork.

I ran backward with my cane pole in order to pull my fish out of the water. But when I landed my catch on the bank, my grandfather took one look at it and growled, "All you got is a carp. Throw it back."

With that background, then, it should come as no surprise that when I read the *Times* story I, too, reacted, "Who in the devil would want a bigger carp?"

I talked to several fishing experts to find out. One, Charles Salter, fishing writer of *The Journal/Constitution* in Atlanta, told me Orientals treat carp as a delicacy.

He even said that during the Vietnam War, Lyndon Johnson sent fish experts to that country to help natives produce more carp.

Mr. Salter did, however, agree there has been some hostility toward the carp in this country and he also said the carp was difficult to clean. ("You have to bleed 'em," he said. Ugh.)

I also read a piece by veteran outdoor writer Charlie Elliot, who defended the carp, saying if prepared correctly it makes a delicious meal and that carp are fun to fish for because they will bite anything, such as doughballs made of everything from cornmeal to powdered crackers, peanut butter, onions, and Jell-O.

Perhaps I could have changed my grandfather's mind about the carp had the *Times* story broken while he was still alive.

"You know the *Times*," I could have said to him. " 'All the news that's fit to print.' "

"That's one thing," my grandfather likely would have said, "but 'all the fish that's fit to eat' is quite another."

Getting Rid of Ants Is No Picnic

I was home visiting the folks in Moreland, Georgia, and my stepfather, H.B., and I walked out into the front yard.

Over near the driveway, I noticed a couple of large anthills.

"I've tried everything I know to get rid of these ants," said my stepfather. "I even put grits on them."

For a second, I thought he had said he put grits on the ants, but you'd have to be about half-addled to do something like that, and H.B. is, without doubt, of sound mind.

I know a lot about grits. I know they are misunderstood. The reason people from regions other than the South don't like grits is they have never had them prepared properly.

They are traveling through the South and stop at a HoJo for breakfast and the waitress serves them grits with their eggs and bacon.

They're probably instant grits to begin with, and I'm sure it's in the Bible somewhere that instant grits are an unholy hybrid of the real thing.

Also, our travelers don't know to put butter on their grits and then stir their eggs and bacon into them and salt and pepper to taste.

So their grits taste awful. And when they return home, they are asked, "Did you have any grits?"

And they say, "The worse thing we ever ate. Almost ruined our trip to Disney World."

But grits on an anthill?

"You didn't really put grits on these ant beds, did you?" I said to my stepfather.

"That's exactly what I said. Putting grits on ant beds is an old remedy for getting rid of ants."

"Giving Northerners unbuttered instant grits is an old remedy for getting rid of tourists, too," I said.

"What's supposed to happen," H.B. went on, "is the ants try to eat the individual little grits and they get so full they explode and die."

I've heard of other old remedies. I know if you put tobacco juice on a bee sting, it will quit hurting.

I know to put a pork chop around an ugly child's neck to get the dogs to play with him, and I know if you bury a dishrag under a full moon your warts will go away.

But, again, grits on an anthill?

So I asked, "How are the grits working on the ants?"

"These ants," answered H.B., "don't seem to be interested in grits."

"Aha!" I said. "They're Northern ants."

"How do you know?"

"Elementary," I said. "They refuse to eat grits, and look how many of them are wearing sandals with black socks."

I told my stepfather not to worry about the ants. They'd be on their way to Disney World in a matter of days.

A Grain of Truth in Straight Talk About Cereal

Let's have some straight talk about cereal. Cereal used to be simple. Your mother put Rice Krispies or Grape-Nuts Flakes on the breakfast table with milk.

You dutifully filled your bowl with each and ate, because that is the way we did things back when children still respected their parents and boys didn't wear earrings and nice girls didn't even kiss on the first date and "going all the way" meant a trip to the state capital.

I never stopped to ask, "Why am I eating this cereal?"

As a matter of fact, I never stopped to ask much of anything in those days. It was against the rules to be too inquisitive, although I did wonder to myself, "What does Ozzie Nelson do for a living?"

I probably saw every episode of *The Adventures of Ozzie and Harriet,* and I don't remember Ozzie ever going to work. He probably sat around the house eating Rice Krispies all day, for all I know.

I stopped eating cereal after I left home. I was tired of it. Same old Rice Krispies. Same old "Snap, crackle and pop," which ceased to be amusing after I turned four. I figured I'd eaten all the cereal I'd ever have to eat.

But after being off cereal for a number of years, something happened. What happened was the word "fiber."

It's a simple little five-letter word that once was used almost exclusively in regard to the textile industry.

But no more.

First there was Euell Gibbons out there in the woods eating berries and nuts and God knows what else, and then came John Denver munching down cereal out in the Rocky Mountains someplace, telling us how important it is we get our daily dose of fiber, which means whatever it is in cereal that allegedly makes one's bowels move regularly.

You don't eat cereal, goes the message, your bowels don't move regularly and you die of about thirty-seven different types of cancer.

That's been hammered in my head so strongly that if I miss a single day without cereal, I call my attorney to make sure my will is in order.

But it's not easy to pick a cereal anymore. Television is filled with commercials boasting the fiber content of dozens of cereals.

And the new cereals don't have names like the cereals I ate as a kid: Rice Krispies, Sugar Pops, Frosted Flakes, Cheerios. Harmless little names.

Today, we are urged to eat cereals with names like Nutra-Grain. Isn't that something they feed to cows out in Nebraska?

And Fiber 1. Sounds like a classification of racing cars. Then there's Product 19. And what happened to products 1 through 18? Inquiring minds want to know.

I've been back on cereal for a while now, because I've gotten the hint, and I want to maintain my health.

But I wonder: Euell Gibbons and Ozzie Nelson are both dead, and John Denver hasn't had a hit song in years.

As much cereal as he apparently eats, I guess he hasn't been able to sit still long enough to write one.

4

RELIGION

We're All Still in God's Waiting Room

The world was supposed to have come to an end recently. In case you haven't noticed, it didn't.

Some sort of religious author had predicted something called "The Rapture" was going to take place, and all believers were going to be whisked off to heaven, while the poor souls who didn't believe were to be left to face seven years of fires, famine, and daily reruns of *The Newlywed Game*.

I'm not certain what went wrong with the prediction, but there must be a lot of angry people out there who believed the end was coming.

There were reports of believers getting rid of their homes and earthly belongings. I even heard of one guy who sold all his Kroger stock.

The next day, fueled by reports of a new Kroger reorganization to fend off a takeover bid, Kroger stock jumped through the ceiling.

"The next time somebody tells me the world is going to end," the unlucky fellow said, "I'm going to wait until it actually happens before I call my broker."

Sound financial advice, indeed.

As for me, I was a little skeptical of the whole thing from the beginning. Somebody is always predicting the world is going to come to an end, but so far it hasn't happened.

There was a man in my hometown, Luther Gilroy, who claimed he was out plowing his field and saw a sign in the sky that said THE END IS NEAR.

Luther let his mule and his cow out of their pens, gave all his chickens away, and climbed on top of his house to await the end.

When it didn't come, he pouted and refused to come down off the roof.

Finally, his wife called the deputy sheriff, who came over and said, "Luther, you idiot, I saw that same sign. It didn't say, 'The end is near.' It said, 'Go drink a beer.' Now come down off that roof before you fall off and break your neck."

I didn't do anything differently on "Doomsday." I went ahead and had breakfast and lunch, tuning in Cable News Network only occasionally to see if it made any sense to make dinner plans.

I even went out and played eighteen holes of golf, and I won a few bucks from my opponent.

He waited for seven o'clock—the precise time the end was supposed to have come to pass—and then wrote me a check.

I'm predicting the world isn't going to come to an end anytime soon. There's too much unresolved, like whether or not Elvis is still alive, Jimmy Swaggart can stay on television, and if there will be another *Rambo* sequel.

I think I will go ahead and cash in some of my frequent-flyer points, though. Remember, I also predicted the Dow would reach three thousand, Bush would pick Kemp, and Jesse would go quietly.

Giving the Bird
to a Turkey

There is nothing like a good fight among Baptists. Baptists are against drinking, dancing, gambling, and most everything else that is fun, but they always seem to enjoy a good fight.

I grew up near the Baptist church in Moreland, Georgia. One year, the church voted to install chimes that would play hymns over the loudspeaker for the townsfolk to enjoy during suppertimes.

One of the members happened to be a turkey farmer, and he claimed the chimes bothered his turkeys during their evening meal and they weren't eating and getting fat so he could sell them to slaughter.

Ugliness ensued. The turkey farmer took to shooting at the loudspeaker on the church steeple in order to silence the chimes.

Other members of the church, meanwhile, often crept into the turkey pens at night, carrying hatchets, which spooked the birds, giving them yet another reason not to eat.

Only after the church steeple had been riddled with bullet holes and most of the turkey farmers' flock had suffered complete nervous breakdowns was the matter settled. The church agreed to play the chimes at an hour that would not interfere with the turkeys' eating habits, and the turkey farmer called off his artillery.

A good time was had by all.

We have another Baptist battle going on presently. A fundamentalist Baptist—a member of the group that enjoys burning books and don't wave at each other at liquor stores—has attacked the leaders of the Baptist-affiliated Mercer University in Macon, Georgia.

The fundamentalist is Lee Roberts, Sr., an Atlanta mortgage banker taken to wearing shiny suits, a Rolex watch, and an onyx ring covered with a cross of diamonds. He has a solid background in fighting against the more liberal of his brethren.

Mr. Roberts mailed a sixteen-page booklet to Baptist ministers, parents of Mercer students, and Mercer trustees in which he denounced Mercer leadership for everything from debauchery, heresy, and failing to outfit Mercer coeds with chastity belts.

Mr. Roberts cited numerous examples of his charges:

- *Playboy* magazine named Mercer as one of the nation's top party schools. (If Mercer students can find a lot of trouble to get into in Macon, then they must at least be honored for their ingenuity.)
- *Playboy* ran photographs of partially nude Mercer coeds. Not only were they missing articles of clothing, their chastity belts appeared to be missing as well.
- The student newspaper has run condom ads, lewd cartoons, and has printed sexually explicit reading material.
- R-rated movies are shown on campus and liquor is served at school functions.

As a result of these sins, Mr. Roberts wants Mercer president Kirby Godsey's and the Mercer trustees' hides. If he doesn't get his way, he says the Georgia Baptist Convention, a real fun group, will stop sending Mercer its $2 million in annual support.

This is one Baptist fight that I, a Methodist, would like to get involved in.

Here's what I would do if I were the Mercer president or a member of the Mercer trustees:

- I would reassure Mercer students they will not see the university turned into a monastery and that it is not for sale at any price—not for $2 million or thirty pieces of silver.
- And I would fight to the death not to allow anybody of Roberts's persuasion to try to set the clock back one hundred years at Mercer University.
- Turkeys like that have a lot in common with condoms. You can see right through them.

Humor out of This World

The good news regarding the recent scandals involving the television evangelists is that they have provided the opportunity for much needed humor.

They have even revived some old material. Remember the joke about Oral Roberts starting his own record company?

It's going around again:

"Hear about Oral Roberts starting a record company?"

"No, what happened?"

"He went out of business. The hole in the middle of his records kept healing shut."

I liked the one about Jerry Falwell running into Jimmy Swaggart in an airport one day.

They began to chat and quite naturally the conversation got around to money.

"How, Brother Falwell," began Brother Swaggart, "do you

decide what part of the money you get from your believers each week goes to the Lord and how much you keep for yourself?"

"Very simple," Brother Falwell explained. "Each week I take all the money my flock has sent in and put it into a large cardboard box. Then I go into my office, where I have a line drawn on the floor. I throw all the money up into the air, and what falls to the left of the line I give to the Lord. What falls on the right I keep."

"Very good," said Brother Swaggart. "I have a similar system of deciding how much I give the Lord and how much I keep. I also go into my office with all the money, and I also throw it up into the air, and whatever the Lord catches he can keep."

I know people who are now admitting publicly they were regular watchers of the PTL Club. They didn't watch for the salvation, however. They watched for the humor.

"Jim and Tammy Faye were the best husband-and-wife comedy team since Burns and Allen, and I miss them," a friend was saying.

"My favorite routine of theirs was when Jim and Tammy Faye both dressed up in sailor suits and Jim begged for money to pay for the water slide at Heritage Village while Tammy Faye cried. After she had cried for a few moments, she looked like Soupy Sales had just hit her in the face with a mascara pie."

"I really miss both of them," my friend continued. "Watching PTL now is nothing like it used to be."

Richard Dortch and Jerry Falwell both look like they're constipated, and I can't stand to watch Jimmy Swaggart. He seems to be in such pain. Maybe he has the same problem as Dortch and Falwell.

I remain convinced humor is just as good for the soul as watching a television evangelist, and I close with the following gems currently making the rounds:

- Did you hear Oral Roberts died? The check bounced.
- How is Tammy Faye Bakker's face like a ski slope? Five inches of base, six inches of powder.
- Did you hear about the television evangelist who is a cross between Jim Bakker and Oral Roberts? If he doesn't have sex within the next two weeks, he is going to die.

Say good night, Tammy Faye.

Pay as You Inter

A minister in England got into trouble recently for preaching a funeral and saying the departed was mean, never did any good, and "won't be missed."

Most ministers wouldn't say anything like that at a funeral for a mass murderer.

The tradition at funerals is to go soft on the guest of honor, although he or she might have been a terrible scoundrel in life.

But why is that? Why should we pretend a person who has just died was not the rascal he or she was, if that happens to be the case?

I remember when Loot Starkins died back home. He was a miserable old tightwad who beat his dogs, growled at small children, wouldn't go to church because he despised people, and, on top of all that, he was a Republican.

Struggling to find a few kind words to say about Loot at his funeral, the minister offered, "We should all remember we can find some good in everybody."

A man stood up in the back of the church and replied, "Loot Starkins didn't have a good bone in his body. He owed me a hundred bucks and I know damn well the old fool died just to get out of paying me."

There also is the matter of the minister comforting the family by saying the loved one has gone on to a better life in heaven.

The preacher back home used that technique for Virgil Crabtree's funeral, but everybody knew Virgil Crabtree couldn't have gone to heaven.

He made and ran bad moonshine, got into a fight every Saturday night at the Moose Club, cursed on Sunday, and refused to bathe regularly.

The preacher might as well have been honest about it and told the family what they already knew anyway, that Virgil couldn't have gotten through the Pearly Gates with a gold American Express card and written recommendations from three of the original disciples.

There's an old story that allegedly is true and it also tells us that honesty is the best policy at a funeral.

Some years ago, the radio announcer for the Chattanooga Lookouts, a minor league baseball team, had some time to kill before broadcasting a game in Memphis, so he rented a car and began driving around the countryside.

He came upon a white-frame church where a funeral was in progress. The announcer, fortified with a few beers, went into the church and took a seat in the first pew.

Several of the deceased's friends were called to the pulpit to say a few words of remembrance. The preacher, figuring anybody in the front row obviously was close to the casketee, called the announcer forward.

"I must be truthful," the announcer began. "I didn't know the gentleman you are remembering here today, but judging from what I've heard so far, he must have been a well-respected and loved individual.

"Obviously," he went on, "I can add nothing to what already has been said, but as long as I'm up here I'd like to say a few words on behalf of the Chattanooga Lookouts."

Tell it all, brother. Tell it all.

Enough Is Enough

During all the mess concerning the television evangelists, I kept wondering what's the Reverend Ike up to these days.

You remember the Rev. Ike? He is a dynamic, suave black man who preaches how God is going to make all his believers rich.

Rev. Ike, with headquarters in Boston and New York, says if you want a new car, send him a few bucks and he'll pray for you and you'll soon have your new car, compliments, I suppose, of Holy Spirit Autos.

Anyway, I now know what the Rev. Ike has been up to lately. The same old thing. Send cash, the Rev. Ike is still saying, and you will receive "help, happiness, love, success, prosperity and more money."

A friend of mine, Roy Brady, got this message in a letter he received from the Rev. Ike. Mr. Brady, who had no intention of sending the Rev. Ike the time of day, passed the letter on to me.

Here was the deal the Rev. Ike was offering Roy Brady.

In the letter, the Rev. Ike sent along what he described as a "blessed, red token string."

Mr. Brady was instructed to hold the string in his hand while reading the Rev. Ike's letter.

"My eyes are filled with tears of joy as I write this letter to you," the Rev. Ike went on.

"I was working and praying for you this morning in the prayer tower and I felt in my heart you needed some extra help this month."

The Rev. Ike further instructed Mr. Brady to put his red token string into his window as soon as possible and to leave it there overnight.

Then he was to mail the string back to the Rev. Ike along with, you guessed it, a "faith donation."

The Rev. Ike said when he received the red string from Mr. Brady he would put it in the prayer tower and in no time at all Mr. Brady would get his health, happiness, love, more money, etc.

This was interesting, too.

"Do not keep this blessed, red token string longer than overnight," the Rev. Ike warned.

"Get it out of your home tomorrow, no later than 8:37 P.M."

What, God closes shop at 8:37 P.M. and doesn't handle any more miracles until the next morning?

We've all had a lot of fun over the last few weeks with Jim Bakker and Tammy Faye and the boys. But do you know how many people are out there, old and ignorant and desperate, who believe the kind of bull the Rev. Ike and his ilk send out to them?

I still don't understand why the sort of letter the Rev. Ike sent to Roy Brady doesn't constitute mail fraud.

We're chasing insider stock traders while overlooking the people who are up in their prayer towers.

You want to send your money somewhere it will do some good, don't send it to these people.

Give it to your own church. Give it to the poor and homeless, give it to the hungry of the world.

Give it to the American Heart Association or the American Cancer Society or to any number of reputable charities.

When the *Charlotte Observer* began coming down heavy on Jim and Tammy Faye and the PTL Club, Jim came up with a motto around which his followers could rally against the heat of the criticism.

"Enough is enough" was that motto.

Damn right, enough is enough. It's time to run these money changers back into the black holes from whence they sprang.

Was It the Lord's Work?

Well, it could have happened . . .

Deputy Sheriff Whitlock was perched behind Kentucky Fried Chicken, birdlike himself, watching for speeders.

Deputy Sheriff Whitlock enjoyed his job, especially watching for speeders behind Kentucky Fried Chicken. He got to doze off occasionally, and Charlene, the girl behind the KFC counter, would bring him out a wing or a leg and a roll and some iced tea each day at lunchtime.

Deputy Sheriff Whitlock had just wiped the grease from the chicken off his mouth when his radar detector nearly jumped out of his car.

He looked up just in time to see one of those fancy 380SL Mercedes convertibles whisk past him as nothing more than a blur. He took one last gulp of tea and threw gravel all over the parking lot as he sped away after the Mercedes in hot pursuit.

"I got me a good 'un, this time!" said the deputy sheriff.

The radar showed the Mercedes traveling 65 in a 40-mph zone. Deputy Sheriff Whitlock rarely saw so bold a speeder.

Most of his collars were little ol' ladies in big Buicks who couldn't see over the dashboard and occasionally ran red lights, or a Roto-Rooter van making an illegal turn.

The deputy roared up behind the Mercedes and turned on his blinking blue lights.

The Mercedes pulled over.

Deputy Sheriff Whitlock got out of his squad car and walked toward the Mercedes, ready for action with his ticket book in hand.

"May I see your driver's license, please?" he said to the man in the Mercedes.

The man, well-dressed and cooperative, handed the officer his license.

After a casual look at the license, the deputy suddenly did a double take and looked back at the name he found there.

"I can't believe it!" he said. "You're Jim Bakker, the television preacher."

"Yes, I am," said the Rev. Bakker, as he flashed his best boyish smile.

"I'm a big fan of yours, and my wife just loves the way Tammy dresses," Deputy Sheriff Whitlock went on.

"You must be one of our partners at PTL," said the Rev. Bakker.

"Damn right," said the deputy, who then asked, "but why were you going so fast?"

"I'm late for my show," the Rev. Bakker answered.

"Well, I guess I can understand that," said the deputy. "The Lord's work can't wait. But you were weaving a little, too, I noticed.

"Say, what's in that bottle in the seat next to you?"

"Nothing but water."

"Water? That don't look like no water bottle. Can I see it?"

The Rev. Bakker handed over the bottle. Deputy Sheriff Whitlock took out the cork and had himself a smell. "Whooo! Rev. Jim," he said, "this ain't water. This is wine."

"Praise Jesus!" the Rev. Bakker shouted. "He's done it again!"

5

THE NEWS

Where No News Is Good News

I recently spent an entire week without any news. It was great.

I was out in the Greek Isles somewhere sailing around and doing very little else and not once did I come into contact with even the slightest bit of news.

I had no idea what was going on in South Korea, with Irangate, or with the latest analysis of how much longer the world population can make it without all of us dying of AIDS.

I became quite relaxed as a result of this. My food also tasted and digested better and the nervous habit I have of wiggling my left foot even went away.

I thought to myself, "I wish everybody could have such an experience."

It's the news that makes most of us worry and get ulcers and do stupid things like running five or six miles in extreme heat.

And you can't escape the news. So you don't read a paper for four or five days, and you avoid evening news broadcasts on television.

Somebody will still walk up to you and say, "Hey, did you read in the paper where the earth is getting hotter and will burn to a crisp sometime between next Monday and the year 3030?"

If you don't have the news to disturb and concern you, your outlook on life, I discovered, improves dramatically.

You can watch the beauty of a sunrise over the Aegean and say to yourself, "Nobody is stupid enough to blow all this up with a bomb."

You really can believe things like that when you're not getting any news.

You can watch three generations—father, his son, and his son—build a boat by hand on some remote island where fishing has fed the inhabitants for hundreds of years and come away convinced maybe there are some things and some people a computer will never replace.

You can eat fresh tomatoes and cucumbers in a taverna with its own garden and forget there is such a thing as fast food or that if you eat too much bacon you can get cancer.

You can take a nap in the middle of the day and not give a damn what latest craziness had been attributed to Oliver North.

You can plunge into the clear sea in some deserted cove and never once consider who's going to get the Democratic nomination for president. (I personally think it's going to wind up being Sam Nunn, but who cares? An octopus could be about to grab your leg.)

You can visit a seven-hundred-year-old monastery and wrap yourself in the quiet sacredness of the place, and never once wonder how many people died that day in some nuthouse holy war.

You can breathe the salt air and feel the spray on your face as your boat chops onward under sail and it matters not that there is a rock song out titled "I Want Your Sex."

You can even look at a nude bather lying on the rocky Aegean shore sunning his buttocks and never once think of Ed Meese.

Then, after all that, you can take leave of that setting and buy the *International Herald Tribune* in the Athens airport and the first thing you read is Oral Roberts is now claiming he has raised the dead.

Film, I suppose, at eleven.

Journalism Gone Bonkers

I was walking through a convenience store and I noticed one of those tabloid newspapers that always have the great headlines.

The lead headline on this particular paper screamed "WWII PLANE FOUND ON MOON!"

This, of course, was rather mild compared to other headlines you see in the world of journalism gone bonkers.

Some of my other favorites over the years have been GIRL, 11, GIVES BIRTH TO CALF!, GHOST OF ELVIS HAUNTS MR. ROGERS!, WOMAN PUREES HUSBAND IN HOME BLENDER!

This is my twenty-third year as a journalist. Some of it has been great fun.

I covered a national political convention once where they gave the press free beer.

I've talked to two presidents, one man who claimed to be Jesus, and another who said he knew who was buried in the Tomb of the Unknown Soldier but was sworn to secrecy.

But there are the slow periods, too. When all you've got cooking is tax reform, high winds in Kansas, and another ballplayer headed for a drug rehab program.

I was thinking as I left the convenience store how much

easier this profession would be if we could do like the tabloids and simply make up the news. That, essentially, is what those publications do. They make up news stories, put big headlines on them, and place them in racks in convenience stores and grocery stores.

And they get away with it because a lot of people with pin-sized brains take this stuff seriously.

There's a lot of things I could write about today: the trouble in Panama, the presidential election, the West Bank, the fall of the dollar—but I'd rather make up some news.

Did you hear Big Foot made a recent appearance on *Soul Train*, for instance?

You didn't know about that?

"Dangdest thing ever," said Lewanda J., a *Soul Train* regular who danced with B.F. "He is a dancin' fool, but I had to watch out he didn't step on my head with one of those big feet."

If you didn't know about Big Foot, you probably didn't hear about the baby who was born in Yonderville, South Dakota, with six heads, either.

Said the proud parents, "We got half them heads named, but we're still working on the other three."

How about the fact that Cleveland recently disappeared from the face of the earth? Heck of a thing. Authorities think it might have been the work of urban planners.

Then there was the episode where a thirty-four-year-old woman from Delores, Texas, married a frog.

"It was between him and that nice goat who lives up the street," she said. "I just hope I haven't leaped into anything too fast."

Did you know that Merv Griffin and Yassir Arafat are the same person? Did you hear that you can lose weight with the new elephant diet? You can eat one elephant a day, but you have to catch your own elephant.

I'd like to go on, but a story just broke that George Bush is actually from Uranus.

See you in the funny papers.

Call Me "MAODWMNSPCG-14HGWS"

I was glancing through the paper the other day and I came across personal ads in the classified section.

Ever read those ads? They're much more interesting than reading the soybean futures on the financial pages, and I lost interest in Dick Tracy years ago.

One ad read, "GWM wants to meet GWM for travel and intimate relationship. Must be nonsmoker."

After some thinking (I'm also brilliant on the Jumble word game, having gotten "UTICRA"—guitar—in fifteen seconds), I figured out what the capital letters in the ads stood for.

"GWM," of course, is a "gay white male," and I'm thinking here's this gay guy who wants to travel and become intimate with another gay guy and he's got to know the facts about AIDS, but what he's concerned about is breathing secondhand smoke from his lover's cigarette.

Another ad read, "SWF wants SWM who's into jazz, the classics, vintage wines, and hiking."

"SWF" and "SWM," I figure, have to stand for "single white female" and "single white male."

"Straight" is possible, too, but let's not get overly immersed in detail, and just who does this SWF think she is kidding here?

Any single white female who has to resort to taking out an ad to find a boyfriend would take a SWM who's into yodeling, *Hustler* magazine, Ripple, and robbing convenience stores.

Still another ad read: "SBM, handsome, athletic, financially secure, wants SBF, 20s, who will be his princess."

If I were a SBF (single black female) I would want to know how this narcissist got his money, and if being his princess meant I'd have to get tied up or do anything involving live animals.

I don't think I'd ever put an ad in the personal section, but if I ever did resort to such a thing, I'm afraid I'd have a difficult time getting all I wanted to say about myself in a few capital letters.

I'm a "DWM," a divorced white male (okay, an oft-DWM). On top of that I'm a "MAODWM," a "Middle-aged-oft-divorced-white-male," and I don't smoke, which makes me a "MAODWMNS."

I'd also like for prospective companions to know I'm a Protestant, a college graduate, a 14-handicap golfer, and I snore, which now has me up to being a "MAODWMNSPCG-14HGWS."

Naturally, I'd also want to point out I'm a dog lover who brushes his teeth regularly, still has his hair, loves egg sandwiches, and often entertains friends by doing a simply marvelous impression of FDR declaring war on the Japanese in 1941.

Now, how are you going to get all that in a classified ad?

If my social life reaches the desperate point, I can always go after the "SWHWs."

Single Waffle House waitresses. They're around twenty-four hours a day and make the best egg sandwiches in town.

b

TEE
TIME

Why I Get Tee'd Off

The only resolution I've made for this year is to stop worrying about all the little things that drive me crazy.

I can handle the big stuff. So what if the president has no idea what the people in charge of our national security are doing? He'd probably just get in the way if he did.

College athletes taking steroids? If the Boz wants to turn green and look like the Incredible Hulk, fine.

I can even deal with secondhand smoke, as long as it's not coming from the roof of my house.

But that annoying, nagging everyday stuff, that's what boils me.

You know what I hate? I hate those little plastic strings that hold tags on new clothes, the ones with the T-shaped ends to keep the tags fastened.

Ever try to get one of those things out of a pair of tennis socks? It can't be done without an acetylene torch, which I never have with me when I'm about to play tennis.

But I have resolved to endure them.

I hate cute messages on telephone recorders, too. Why do people think they have to be funny?

"Hi, this is Arnold. Heard the one about the guy who walks up to a man standing by a dog?

" 'Does your dog bite?' he asked the man, who replies 'No.' So the guy reaches down to pet the dog, and the dog takes two of his fingers clean off.

" 'I thought you said your dog doesn't bite,' the first guy said. And the other guy answers, 'That's not my dog.'

"Thought you'd like that one. Now, at the tone, please leave your, etc. etc."

I don't have time for silly jokes when I try to reach somebody on the phone, but I'm going to try to handle them and stop leaving messages that say, "This is Carl Meggenfuss at the IRS. Call me immediately, or else."

I'm not going to get mad anymore when television newscasters joke with one another and make "happy talk."

I'm going to learn to handle it when I switch through the channels with my remote control device and discover *The Newlywed Game* is still on the air and nobody has shot Bob Eubanks.

I'm not going to have a stroke when I expressly tell the pizza place, "No anchovies," and thirty minutes later the pizza arrives covered with those godawful little hairy things, whatever they are.

I'm not going to become livid with rage anymore when I'm playing behind a woman on the golf course and she continues to attempt to hit the ball after a dozen would-be strokes.

I am going to handle it when I drive through a McDonald's and order a hamburger and some fourteen-year-old asks, "Would you like french fries with that?" I simply will say, "No," not "If I'd wanted the bleeping fries I would have asked for them, pimpleface."

I'm not going to pull my phone out of the wall anymore when I get computerized calls, lose control when somebody steals my Sunday paper, or sulk and go into the fetal position when the water pressure in the shower is lousy in the hotel room for which I am paying $150 a day.

That's me. Mr. Calm.

Women. Why don't they have their own damn golf courses.

My Handicap:
Women Golfers

Judging from my mail, phone calls, and random death threats, I get the distinct feeling many women golfers were not happy with my recent suggestion that women have their own golf courses so they wouldn't have to worry about slowing down men golfers.

Wrote "Disgusted," from Orlando, Florida, "I'd like to take a three iron and stick it . . ."

Scribbled "Outraged," from Odessa, Texas, "The same goes for me."

Lady golfers where I play burned a sand wedge in front of my locker, and my secretary, the lovely and talented Miss Wanda Fribish, who is also an officer in the 303rd Bombardier Wing of the National Organization for Livid Women, said, "Die, scrud!" as she threw her daggerlike letter opener at me.

Luckily, I was able to dodge her missile. It stuck in the photograph of the October playmate that hangs on my wall.

Perhaps I should attempt to clear up my stand on women on the golf course:

First, there are many, many women who can beat me playing golf. I am to golf what Muammar Qaddafi is to world peace.

Who I'm talking about are the female versions of me, the lady hackers. They are the ones who slow down play, and here is why.

When the male high-handicapper reaches a score of double bogey or triple bogey and he still doesn't have the ball in the hole, he avoids further embarrassment by moving on to the next hole so as not to slow down golfers behind him. Not so with many women high-handicappers. They are resolved to get the ball into the hole regardless of how many strokes it takes.

I was playing behind a woman at a resort course recently. After she took two hours to complete the first six holes, I counted her strokes on the seventh.

She made a 26. It was a par 3.

Men and women could get along on the same golf course if women simply would PUT THE DANG BALL IN THEIR POCKETS AND MOVE ON AFTER THEIR SCORE REACHES DOUBLE DIGITS.

This will never happen, of course, which is why women should have their own golf courses so they can hack the ball around as long as their hearts desire. Women have their own rest rooms and bridge clubs, don't they?

To close, a little golf story:

Guy is playing golf with his wife and slices his tee shot into the rough behind the barn.

His wife says, "Why don't I open the door and you hit the ball through the barn toward the green?"

The guy tries it, but the ball hits something inside the barn and caroms off and hits his wife in the head, killing her.

A year later, the same guy is playing with a friend, and he slices the ball behind the same barn.

His friend says, "Why don't I open the door and you hit the ball through the barn toward the green?"

"No way," says the guy. "Last time I tried that here I made a seven."

As far as Ms. October is concerned, she was hit by the letter opener in such a location that she certainly won't be playing golf anytime soon.

Roughly Speaking, I Play Golf

Recall that on the second sudden-death play-off hole of the Masters golf tournament (on April 12, 1987), Larry Mize chipped in a birdie from off the green to win the tournament from Greg Norman, who is the best golfer on the planet.

Norman had no recourse but to move on to the next tournament, the Heritage Classic at the Harbour Town Golf Links at Hilton Head, where something else happened to him that was traumatic. He had to play in the Pro-Am with me as one of his partners.

Since I have no grandchildren, let me tell you about my golf game. I began playing golf when I was sixteen at a lovely course near my native Moreland, Georgia.

The course had a number of interesting touches. You teed off next to a barn, you often had to shoot over cows grazing on the course/pasture, and if your ball landed in a substance cows are famous for (besides milk), you got a free drop.

I played golf until I was twenty-two, and then I quit due to a lack of talent and took up tennis.

I played tennis every day for the next sixteen years. About a year ago, however, I awakened one morning and was no longer able to brush my teeth with my right hand because my shoulder was hurting so badly from playing tennis every day for sixteen years.

So, fool that I am, I started playing golf again. I presently carry a 14 handicap, hook the ball miserably, and recently missed a three-inch putt.

Back to Greg Norman. What a nice man. He signed about

three thousand autographs and posed for at least that many pictures during our round.

As I watched him smile his way through all that, I thought of a young sportswriter trying to interview baseball's Darryl Strawberry of the Mets during spring training. The kid asked Strawberry a simple question.

"Out of my face," is how Strawberry answered him.

Norman had a bad round in the Pro-Am, he shot 5 over par. I lost control of my game and birdied the fifth hole.

On number six, I chipped in from off the green for another birdie.

"I've seen that shot before," said Norman, referring to Mize's winning chip against him in Augusta.

"And it was going the same speed," he added, referring to the fact that both Mize's shot and my shot would still be rolling had they not gone into the hole.

Playing golf with Greg Norman and making back-to-back birdies is one of the highlights of my life.

And who would have thought such a thing would happen to me years ago back home when a cow once mooed during my backswing and I hit my shot into the pigpen, where a large hog promptly ate my ball.

"The Snake Rule"
of Golf

There is only one way to reach Daufuskie Island, South Carolina, and that is by boat.

I boarded on nearby Hilton Head Island for the forty-five-minute trip over to Daufuskie.

In the last century, there was a working plantation here by the name of Melrose. A facsimile of that plantation has been recarved from the wooded thickets.

Melrose now offers its members peaceful, quiet, gracious hospitality, not to mention a beautiful inn, cottages on the beach, horseback riding, tennis, and golf on a Jack Nicklaus course.

It was the golf that lured me there. On the par-4 fourteenth, I hooked my drive into the woods. As I drove off in my cart in search of it, my partner said, "Be careful. They've been seeing a lot of snakes lately."

Snakes are right up there with the things I fear most. Lightning is on that list. So is flying in bad weather at night, the dentist and revenge-minded ex-wives.

"What kind of snakes have they been seeing?" I asked my fellow competitor.

"Rattlesnakes, I guess," he said.

I don't know why I asked that silly of a question. As far as I'm concerned, a snake is a snake. I didn't pay enough attention in Boy Scouts to be able to determine when I step on a snake whether it is going to bite me, coil around me and squeeze me to death, or talk about all the rats it has been eating lately.

"If they ain't got shoulders," my boyhood friend and idol, Weyman C. Wannamaker, Jr., used to say, "I don't want to be near them."

Weyman's uncle had frightened him about the dreaded "cottonmouth water rattler."

"My uncle says that's the meanest snake there is," Weyman explained.

"They'll follow you home and wait for you to come out of the house the next morning."

"Do you think it's safe to go into the woods after my ball?" I asked my partner, as I reminded myself golf balls cost only $2.50.

"Just be careful around thick brush and fallen logs," he said.

I drove my cart into the woods and was about to get out when I noticed all I could see around me was thick brush and fallen logs.

"One other thing!" my partner yelled to me. "Snakes climb up trees, sometimes, and they can fall off on your head."

I might have been able to deal with thick brush and the fallen logs. The part about a snake falling on my head did it, however. I declared my ball lost, took the necessary penalty, and from that point on played by the "snake rule," which clearly states, "Any player who hits a ball anywhere there might be a snake can forget about that ball and drop another in the fairway with no penalty."

I was at Melrose for four wonderful days and, after invoking the snake rule, remained out of the woods and never saw snake one.

My partner, meanwhile, had to play golf with his wife one day.

"She went into the woods on eleven and saw a snake," he explained. "Best thing that ever happened to me."

"What do you mean by that?" I asked.

"The minute she stopped running," he said, "she gave up golf—forever."

The Course of True Golf

Forget the U.S. Open and all that splendid play by the pro golfers and all that money they won and come with me to Winston-Salem, North Carolina, and the golf tournament known simply and elegantly as the Crosby.

It is whatever happened to the Bing Crosby tournament in California that drew the stars and the game's top players for so many years.

The late crooner had indicated that if there came a time that less than 50 percent of the proceeds of his tournament were going to charity, it should be halted, moved, or somehow altered to return to its roots as an event held primarily to help the less fortunate.

The demands for a large purse for the pros finally did deplete the charitable funds, and Crosby's widow, Kathryn, packed the whole thing up and moved it to Burmuda Run Country Club. The tournament raises 8 million for charity.

I was invited to play this year. It was an incredible experience. For four days, I played between the ropes, just like the stars of the PGA.

The Saturday crowd was estimated at over twenty thousand. I, a 14-handicapper who shouldn't be that low, hit a screaming three-iron twelve feet from the pin on the watery seventeenth hole in front of five thousand people.

When I arrived at the green to applause just like at the Masters, I did my best Jack Nicklaus smile and waved.

I missed the putt, but I made par, and it was bigger than the time in high school I hit the pop fly that rolled into the weeds by the concession stand and before the ball could be found, I was around the bases for the winning run.

I also topped a few off the tee, left one in the trap on eighteen, and lost my player's badge and was nearly thrown off the course by a security guard, who said with a sneer, "You don't look like no golfer."

I also got to meet a lot of famous people. Bob Hope was there. I shook his hand.

I also met Oprah Winfrey. (She didn't play golf. They didn't have a cart that big.)

McLean Stevenson, Claude Atkins, Efrem Zimbalist, Jr., football's Dick (Night Train) Lane, and Jim McMahon, the goofy quarterback from the Chicago Bears, left on the same plane I did.

I also played a round with Jim Palmer as my partner. Jim Palmer is the former pitcher for the Baltimore Orioles who now shows up on billboards wearing nothing but his Jockey underwear.

Women love Jim Palmer.

"You're absolutely gorgeous," one woman said to him at the sixth.

"Jim Palmer!" exclaimed another at the tenth. "I didn't recognize you with your clothes on."

It went on like that all day, and I, quite frankly, got a little tired of it. It was difficult to putt with a large group of women offering up various mating calls.

Finally, however, one woman did say to me, "Lewis, what kind of underwear do you have on?"

"Not any," I replied, leaving her eating the dust of my golf cart.

7

MAN'S BEST FRIEND

My Dog, the Genius

Newsweek magazine recently came out with a cover story entitled "How Smart Are Animals?"

Pretty smart, concluded the reporters, who told of chimps who know sign language, a horse that could count, and pigeons with remarkable memories.

I wasn't surprised to find out animals know as much as they do because I live with Catfish, the black Lab, whose intelligence often is astounding.

Even when he was a puppy, he was bright. When he committed an indiscretion on my living-room rug, I said to him, sternly, "Catfish, never do that on my living-room rug again!"

Sure enough, the next time he didn't go on the living-room rug. He went on the rug in the den.

He also learned at a very early age that if he kept whining, no matter how long I ignored him, I finally would give in and share the food on my plate with him. He's especially fond of pizza.

As he got older, Catfish became even smarter. He discovered that twice a week, at approximately 6 A.M., a guy shows up in a truck to take away my garbage.

After that, at the precise moment the garbage truck drove into my driveway, Catfish would come to my bed and bark directly into my ear at a decibel level only slightly lower than a train wreck to awaken me to the fact a stranger was making off with our garbage.

It is only recently Catfish stopped doing that. Once he heard the Supreme Court had ruled a person's garbage is not private, he figured why bother protecting ours any longer.

Catfish's vocabulary also amazes me.

He knows the word "go," for instance. When I say that word, regardless of context, he immediately races to the garage and scratches on my car door. My dog is making Earl Scheib, the famous car painter, a fortune.

Catfish also knows the word "no."

Whenever I say that word, it's a signal to ignore me completely.

Catfish even knows the word "Domino's." He hears that, he knows there's pizza involved, and he drools on my trouser leg.

What Catfish also knows is how to get to me. He does it with those eyes.

How do dogs know they can get anything they want if they just look at you with those sad, loving eyes that ask, "What about me?" and plead, "Please don't go."

Catfish does it to me when I leave him. Those eyes.

"I'll be back in three days," I say.

Those eyes.

"I've got to go. It's business."

Those eyes.

"Okay, you can invite all your friends over for pizza and moon-howling while I'm gone. I'll call Domino's from the airport."

It's tough living with an animal who's smart enough to know a sucker when he sees one.

Going Nuts Over Squirrels

My dog, Catfish, the black Labrador, has been trying unsuccessfully for some time to catch a squirrel in the backyard, and I am concerned this failure eventually will lead him to a nervous breakdown, or even worse.

I have a great number of trees in my backyard, and countless squirrels cavort among them. When Catfish is outside and spots a squirrel, he immediately dashes after it.

I think the squirrels have taken to tantalizing him. They allow Catfish to get just beyond striking distance, and then they dash away and up a tree and look down at my frustrated dog and laugh at him.

Catfish returns from squirrel chasings with a pained, disappointed look on his face. I think he has become obsessed with catching at least one squirrel.

I've tried to trick him into thinking he has caught one. I bought a stuffed squirrel and put it in the yard. Catfish spotted it and attacked. When it didn't run away, he became suspicious. He wasn't dealing with a bona fide squirrel here, and brought it into the house and laid it at my feet, as if to say, "Nice try, Dad, but if it's not the real thing, I'm not interested."

Even if the frustration of coming up empty time and again doesn't make Catfish loony, there is also the problem of what happens when my dog is inside my house and sees a squirrel on the outside.

The back of my house is a series of glass doors, which remain closed most of the time. Catfish has not figured out the theory of glass. He sees a squirrel outside and goes dashing for it and runs into the glass at approximately 65 mph.

"You can't run through glass," I tell him after he has regained consciousness. He gives me that pained, disappointed look again, along with his flattened nose and crossed eyes.

I'm torn here, as one might imagine. I want my dog to live a happy, healthy life and not become brain-damaged. Perhaps, I have thought, if he were to catch just one lousy squirrel, he would be free of this obsession.

On the other hand, I don't want any harm to come to any of the squirrels who live in my backyard. They're cute little boogers, and I enjoy watching them run around in the grass and straw looking for whatever it is squirrels look for.

This experience—and dilemma—has taught me to have a great deal of appreciation for the order of nature.

Dogs naturally chase squirrels, but squirrels are naturally faster than dogs. They scamper up trees to get away from dogs, who have no earthly idea how to climb a tree.

Glass doors, on the other hand, are not a part of the natural order of things.

I simply hope that if one day Catfish crashes headfirst into another one in hot pursuit of a squirrel and suffers a fatal injury, he will somehow know it was the door, not the squirrel, his avowed enemy, who killed him.

The Stranger and the Lost German Shepherd

B.A. and Nancy are close and dear friends of mine. They came to visit for a couple of days and brought their dog, Fang, a female German shepherd.

Fang and my dog, Catfish, the black Lab, could cavort in my fenced backyard. They are old and devoted friends.

B.A. couldn't have picked out a worse name for Fang. She might be the sweetest dog I've ever known.

Fang weighs a ton, but she still wants to sit in your lap. She is calm and obedient and knows her place much better than Catfish knows his.

B.A. has had Fang ten years. He got her in a rather lonely part of his life. Divorced men often go out and buy themselves dogs.

I've said it often, but it remains true: The thing about a dog is, you can come home at any hour, in any condition, and the dog cares not. He, or she, is just glad to see you.

Fang got out of my backyard by digging out from under the fence. Catfish followed her, but he walked to my front porch and waited for somebody to come home.

Fang split for parts unknown.

I felt guilty about it.

"She's done this before," B.A. said. "I just hope she hasn't been run over and hasn't been picked up by somebody who'll mistreat her."

We combed the neighborhood. We even knocked on doors. We called animal control. But no Fang.

"Don't give up," I said to my friends when they had to leave. "She's got her rabies tag and maybe somebody has taken her in and will get in touch with you."

"I guess we need a miracle now," said B.A. "It's been seventy-two hours."

A stranger saw this beautiful German shepherd as she wandered the streets.

He called to the dog and the dog walked over to him. He petted the dog and got the idea she was lost.

He took the dog home with him. He fed her and gave her a warm place to sleep and then got on the horn and started trying to locate the dog's owner.

It took him three days, but—thanks to the rabies tag—he traced B.A. and Nancy.

They drove back immediately and picked up Fang.

"I thought she was going to have a heart attack when she saw us," B.A. said.

"To get to where the man picked her up, she had to cross a lot of busy streets in Friday rush-hour traffic.

"It's a miracle she didn't get run over. It's also a miracle," he went on, "that somebody who obviously cared about dogs and people found her and took her in and then went to the trouble to find us."

It would have been a tough Christmas for B.A. if they'd lost Fang for good.

"She's been with me a long time," he said. "It was killing me to think I'd never see her again."

So, a nice, warm Christmas story. Man and dog reunited, thanks to the kindness of a stranger.

By the way, after the experience with Fang, I found this football made of rawhide that dogs like to chew, and I'm giving it to Catfish for Christmas.

I think I'll throw in a box of dog biscuits, too, and

maybe even some bones from a friend's steak restaurant.

For all my faults, I love my dog. Heaven's got to be at least a little impressed by that.

My Dog, the Star

It's going to sound like I made all this up, but I promise I didn't.

I recently received an inquiry from the good people of Scottsboro, Alabama, regarding their First Annual Catfish Festival.

Scottsboro is a lovely riverside village in north Alabama.

The Catfish Festival will feature arts-and-crafts displays and various other activities, such as contests for catfish-skinning and catfish-cooking.

People are expected to come from as far away as Haleyville and Boaz to attend.

When I saw the date in the letter, I realized I had another commitment and couldn't possibly appear in Scottsboro. Then I read further and realized it wasn't me they wanted in Scottsboro, it was my dog.

My dog, a black Lab, is named Catfish. I'm not sure why I named him that. It just seemed a great name for a dog. Certainly better than something like Buster, Rattler, Old Bullet, or Blackie.

I have written often of Catfish. Once, I wrote how he drinks out of the toilet.

A woman wrote back and said, "Of all things. Only riffraff doesn't keep the lid on their toilet shut."

I closed all the lids on the toilets. Catfish learned to lift them with his nose.

I have also written of Catfish's continuing fruitless pursuit of the hundred thousand or so squirrels in my yard and how intelligent he is to awaken me at six-thirty in the morning when the guy comes to steal our garbage again.

"We would love to have your dog Catfish as a special guest of the festival," the letter said. "He will be introduced at noon at the Goose Pond Amphitheatre."

I talked it over with Catfish, and he wants a shot at this.

"It could be my big break," he said. "Lassie was discovered doing tricks for quarters on a Hollywood street corner."

I have given my okay for Catfish's first public gig. His aunt Louise is going to accompany him to Scottsboro.

I have warned Catfish about certain things he cannot do while appearing in public.

We know what one of these things is. It nearly ruined the career of UGA, the bulldog mascot of the University of Georgia.

"I wouldn't do that," said Catfish.

"See that you don't," I said. "I couldn't take the embarrassment."

I also cautioned Catfish to watch whom, what, and where he sniffs, not to try to eat any of the geese in the Goose Pond, and, by all means, not to chase any cars.

He caught one once and chewed up the tires.

I wonder if Brooke Shields's mother ever felt this proud and excited.

Leading a Dog's Life

A great number of you have been kind enough to ask how my dog, Catfish, the black Lab, fared as the guest of honor at the recent First Annual Catfish Festival in Scottsboro, Alabama.

For those who might not have read earlier, Catfish's aunt Louise drove him over to Scottsboro for the festivities, which was Catfish's first public appearance.

When Aunt Louise returned with him that evening, she couldn't wait to tell me.

"Your dog was wonderful," she said.

"He didn't embarrass me or the corporation?" I asked.

"Not in the least," she said.

You never know about a rookie at his first gig. He could have become nervous and bitten someone, committed an indiscretion during the parade, or chased the 4:15 Greyhound from Birmingham.

"He was a perfect gentleman," said Aunt Louise. "He let all the children pet him, he sat on command and never whined or barked once."

"Did the people seem to like him?" I asked.

"They loved him. He got to ride in a police car with the siren on, he appeared on two television shows, and they gave me a key to the city with his name on it."

This could be the start of an entire new career for Catfish.

Previously, by trade, he's been a shoe chewer, door scratcher, and a squirrel chaser.

He grew out of his shoe chewing and now has his own door through which he comes and goes as he pleases.

He has remained ever vigilant on squirrel patrol, however. Every day of his life, he chases squirrels.

He's never come close to catching one because they all run up trees, but doggedly, if you will, he continues his efforts.

But where might his new public career take him?

To other such festivals, of course. Also to shopping-center openings; used car sales-o-ramas, Moose Club barbecues, and perhaps even to a hog-calling contest or at least a rat killing.

After that perhaps he could catch on with a beer company like those other dogs, or appear in a dog food commercial.

(On second thought, I hate dog food commercials. We all know the dogs are starved when they finally get a bowl of dog food put in front of them, and how does Ed McMahon know Alpo tastes all that good? Has he ever eaten any of it?)

At the moment, I'm also talking to Carson and Letterman. Earl Carson and Marvin Letterman, two guys who want Catfish to appear at the annual Red Bug Roundup in Itchlikehell, West Virginia.

I'm also negotiating with a man who wants Catfish to become national spokesdog for Sooper Dooper Doggie Scooper. A product dog owners especially need, lest our sidewalks become unwalkable.

I do intend, however, to bring Catfish along slowly. Too much too soon is a dangerous thing. That's why I told him he could keep the cigar he came home smoking last night.

"But that gold chain," I said, "has got to go."

A Deuce No Longer Wild

Dee and Jimmy, who are my friends, own a rather large black Lab named Deuce, who has become somewhat of a legend in their hometown.

Nobody is quite certain just how many puppies Deuce has fathered over the years, but the number likely would be astounding.

Deuce, put quite frankly, is one of the greatest lovers in the history of dogdom.

That's caused a lot of problems for Dee and Jimmy over the years.

Not so long ago, Deuce fell in lust with a female pit bull, of all things. He climbed a high fence to have his way with her and was noticed leaving the scene by the pit bull's owner.

He recognized Deuce and called Dee and Jimmy, and an arrangement was made to have the vet to make certain the pit bull didn't turn up with pup.

The pit bull's owner built a higher fence to protect his female.

Deuce came back a week later and scaled the fence, and we're still waiting to see what you get if you cross a black Lab with a pit bull.

My guess is a pit bull who'd rather read *Penthouse* than *Soldier of Fortune*. But Dee and Jimmy gave me the news the other day.

"Deuce's days as a lover are over," Dee said.

"And Jimmy's agreed with this?"

"He says he hates to do it because Deuce has a reputation to uphold, but he's agreed we should have Deuce fixed. He just says he'll never be able to look him in the eye again."

We talked a little about the fact that there are a lot of unwanted animals in the world and that there is a movement afoot for pet owners to be aware of this and to take the necessary steps to keep down the number of strays and unwanteds.

It's a sad thing to see a stray dog or cat terribly undernourished wandering a neighborhood in search for food.

In cities and towns, so many of them get picked up by the animal-control people and subsequently put to death.

"There's something else, too," said Dee. "It got to the point where our neighborhood wasn't enough for Deuce. He began wandering all over town.

"There's a busy highway just a few miles from us, and Deuce would cross it on his way to see some of his girlfriends.

"We really love that dog and we want him around for a long time. Maybe after he's fixed, he will stay around closer to home and won't have as much of a chance to get run over."

I had my own dog, Catfish, another black Lab, fixed a couple of years ago, for the same reason.

I told him I was sending him to the vet for a cholesterol check.

Still, you hate to see any great career come to an end. First, John Holmes, the porno-film star who claimed to have had sex with fourteen thousand different women, up and dies, and now ol' Deuce will no longer be on his ever-vigilant prowl.

A moment of silence, if you will, for the both of them.

Barking Up the
Wrong Tree

I've done a lot of nice things for my dog Catfish, the black Lab.

I allow him to sleep in my house on a dog bed I ordered out of the L. L. Bean catalog.

I buy him dog biscuits and chew toys, and he often gets leftovers from the table. I gave him a banana once. He ate it.

When Catfish wants out of the house, he goes to the door and barks. I leave whatever I'm doing and open the door for him.

When he wants back in, he scratches on the door from the outside and I open it for him.

Then I read an advertisement in a magazine for Alpo Lite. You've read that correctly.

The Alpo dog food people have come out with a new product, Alpo Lite, which according to the ads gives the dog "100 percent nutrition and 25 percent less calories than regular canned dog food."

Diet dog food is what we're talking about here. We've got diet soft drinks, diet beer, diet everything, and now we've got a dog food for dogs who want to watch their figures.

I'm drawing the line here. I'm not going to buy Catfish diet dog food.

In the first place, he doesn't have a weight problem. That's because he spends each day chasing squirrels.

He's never caught a squirrel and apparently never will, but he keeps trying and is in good shape for all that exercise.

Also, I can't see buying a special blend of dog food for a dog that has a gastronomical system that can handle anything.

Catfish is four. During his lifetime, he has eaten the following:

- Four pairs of my eyeglasses
- Two television remote-control devices
- Numerous pairs of shoes
- Various sticks
- An Andy Rooney hardback book
- A cassette of Nat King Cole not available in stores I bought off television
- A wicker chair
- A golf ball
- An entire bag of miniature Snickers bars, bag and wrappers included

And the Alpo people think I'm going to go out and buy Alpo Lite because I'm concerned about my dog getting 25 percent less calories than he gets in his regular canned dog food?

Dog food advertising gets on my nerves anyway. They put down a bowl of dog food on television and the dog dives right in. That's probably because they haven't fed the dog in three days.

Otherwise, if the dog is like mine, he has to smell the dog food for thirty minutes in order to stall for something better off the table.

If nothing comes as a result of his waiting, whining, drooling, and looking at you with those eyes, he might eat his dog food. But not while you're looking.

As for Catfish, how can I worry about his figure when there is an even greater concern? Ever since he ate my Nat King Cole tape, he barks to the tune of "Ramblin' Rose."

8

THEY CALL HIM BUBBA

His Name Is
Nobody's Business

A man walked up to me at a public gathering recently and asked if he could discuss a problem.

"Please continue," I said.

"All my life," he began, "I've had the nickname 'Bubba.' I'm not sure how I got it, but it's what my parents, brothers and sisters, teachers, and friends have always called me.

"My real name is Tom, but very few people know that," he went on.

"And the problem?" I asked.

"I can't be specific here," he said, "but I took a job with a national firm and my boss says I can't use the name Bubba anymore.

"He said it's bad for business to have somebody named Bubba calling on customers. He says Bubba sounds redneck and juvenile and he has insisted I now go by Tom.

"I hate Tom, I'm Bubba. What should I do?"

I must admit this was the first time I had heard of someone being forced to change his name by management for business purposes.

Should a company, or a company executive, have the right to ask such a thing of an employee?

Let's consider this in depth:

The name Bubba does conjure an initial reaction that there

might be a pickup truck involved somewhere, one with muddy tires, a Confederate flag decal on the back window, and a bumper sticker that says I'LL GIVE UP MY GUN WHEN THEY PRY MY COLD, DEAD FINGER OFF THE TRIGGER.

On the other hand, Bubba certainly could be a term of endearment, a little sister's pronunciation of the word "brother," for instance. And Bubba even has its place in modern literature and culture.

Pat Conroy's "Bear" called all the cadets an endearing "Bubba" in Conroy's brilliant *The Lords of Discipline.*

There is also Bubba Smith, the former football player who now bites open beer cans in television commercials.

But would anybody have a problem doing business with a man named Bubba?

I can only speak for myself, but I think I could deal with a Bubba and probably have more in common with him than with a man named Raoul or Tripp.

I would go to a bank to take out a loan from a Bubba, and I'd even have a Bubba for a lawyer. I figure the jury could warm up to a man with a name like that.

Plus, I think that somewhere in the Constitution it probably says an American has the right to have just about any name he or she pleases. Otherwise, Liberace would have been in big trouble. And what would happen to poor Fennis Dembo, the Wyoming basketball player?

I told the man to tell his boss he'd see him in court if he gave him any more trouble about being called Bubba.

For the record, I also asked, "What's your boss's name?"

"Melvin," he said. "But around the office we call him Stinky."

The "Bubba" Stereotype

For years I have attempted to enlighten those individuals who hold biased and ill-based opinions about the name "Bubba."

Most think men named Bubba are nothing more than ignorant swine who wear caps with the names of heavy-equipment dealers on the front, shoot anything that moves, listen to music about doing bodily harm to hippies, and put beer on their grits.

There may be Bubbas who fit the above description, but there are plenty who don't.

Earlier, I wrote of a man—college educated, with no tobacco-juice stains on his teeth—whose family had always referred to him as Bubba.

"I got that name," he explained, "because my baby sister couldn't say brother. She called me Bubba."

The man's problem was that he had taken a job with some sort of high-tech corporation, and his boss insisted he drop the name Bubba because he felt clients wouldn't respect a man with such a name.

Our Bubba refused to use any other name, however, and became quite successful with his new company and wound up with his former boss's job. The former boss now refers to his old employee as "Mr. Bubba."

Anyway, I happened to pick up a back issue of *Southerner* magazine recently, and on the very front cover were the following words:

"Bubba! You don't have to be dumb, mean, fat, slow, white or male to be one!"

I turned to page 37 and began to read:

"Of all the Southern stereotypes," the story began, "the one that answers to 'Bubba' is probably the least flattering."

The article went on to do portraits of eight Bubbas. Do any of the following fit the typical "Bubba" stereotype?

- *Keith (Bubba) Taniguchi:* Attorney, Austin, Texas. Full-blooded Japanese. Into Zen.
- *John (Bubba) Trotman:* State director of the USDA's Agricultural Stabilization and Conservation Service, Montgomery, Alabama. On people moving into Alabama: "At first, they say, 'Alabama, that's Tobacco Road. Then, you can't blow them out of Alabama with a cannon.' "
- *Efula (Bubba) Johnson:* Narcotics officer, Savannah, Georgia. Mr. Johnson is a large black man, and he carries a large gun.
- *Walter (Bubba) Smith:* Minister, Ashdown, Arkansas. Claims no relation to Bubba Smith of football and beer commercial fame.
- *James (Bubba) Armstrong:* Surgeon, Montgomery, Alabama. Careful poking fun at anybody who knows his way around a scalpel.
- *Paula (Bubba) Meiner:* Owns a barbecue joint in Winter Park, Florida. Nice lady.
- *Bernard (Bubba) Meng, III:* State administrator for U.S. Senator Ernest Hollings, Columbia, South Carolina. He's "Little Bubba." Dad was "Big," etc.
- *Kyle (Bubba) Patrick:* Elementary school student, Auburntown, Tennessee. He wants to be a basketball player when he grows up.

One more thing: The University of Georgia veterinary school recently produced the state's first test-tube calf, a Holstein bull weighing one hundred pounds.

They named him Bubba. What else?

9

THE TROUBLE WITH TEENAGERS

Suggested Courses for Today's Teenager

Education Secretary William Bennett decided a while back that high schools aren't tough enough academically, and he has suggested that it might take some students five or six years to graduate, rather than the customary four.

Secretary Bennett suggests high school students take the following courses:

Four years of English; three years each of science, math, and social studies; two years of a foreign language; two years of physical education; and one semester each of art history and music history.

The primary reason younger people don't trust older people is because older people sit around and try to figure out how to make life more difficult for younger people than it already is.

High school isn't tough enough?

When you're fifteen, you're lucky just to be able to dress yourself each morning and locate the school.

Plus, there are all sorts of things to worry about as a teenager without some bureaucrat in Washington trying to put you through Harvard when you're barely housebroken.

You've got to worry about getting your driver's license,

a date for the prom, and tickets for the next heavy-metal concert.

On top of that, your homeroom teacher has it in for you because your earring jingles during quiet period, your father is a narc, and your face is covered with zits.

This is not to say there shouldn't be changes in our high schools. For years I have called upon educators to revamp the curriculum to fit modern times and each student's particular interests and needs.

For instance, they made me take algebra in high school.

"But I'm never going to use this," I pleaded.

"You never know," said my teacher.

I did know, and I was right. I have been out of high school twenty-four years, and not once has algebra come up.

Teaching kids to read and to write and to count a little is important, but high schools also should offer some practical courses that would help students as they join the adult world. I'd like to see a few of these courses taught:

- *How to Get Up in the Morning Without Your Mother Making You.* Self-motivation is something some people have to learn.
- *Dressing for Success.* Law firms do not hire young men wearing earrings or young women with orange hair.
- *How to Speak the English Language.* Like, you know, it's, like, important.
- *Highway Sanity.* Every time you get behind the wheel of a car, don't try to see how fast the car will go. The morgue is, like, a totally boring place.
- *How to Drink Sensibly and Not Throw up on Your Date.* Very important if one is to improve socially.
- *Economics.* Your parents are going to cut you off one of these days. Learn to cope with being in charge of your own survival.

- *Getting Even.* Just hold on a few more years and you can get back at all the adults who made your life miserable by doing the same thing to your own kids.

Life isn't fair, my young friends, but it has its moments.

Why Teachers Play Hooky

Recruiting season for top high school football players is over.

Young men who were offered scholarships have made their choices as to which institutions of higher or lower learning they will attend in the fall.

Due to the heightened academic and character requirements for incoming athletes at most universities, however, some athletes who would have been eligible for signing under last year's requirements were not eligible this year.

I have managed to obtain a list of some of the high school athletes who would have been able to sign had they not been boneheads and social outcasts.

Here are some of the examples from the list:

- *Marvin Toodler,* wide receiver, Corn Silk, Nebraska: Caught 417 touchdown passes and two known venereal diseases during his high school career.

  Unfortunately, when he took his SAT exam, that's all

he did. Sat. Marvin now plans to work for his father, Mr. Toodler, in the family worm-farm business.

• *Leon (Neon) Devon,* running back, Corpus Christi, Texas: What made recruiters suspicious that Leon might be academically deficient was the questionnaire he sent back to interested schools. On each questionnaire, he not only misspelled his name, he also doodled in the margins with a yellow crayon and listed his home town as "Korpus Krispy."

Plans to remain in Texas and seek work repairing anvils.

• *Norman Glovenmeyer III,* quarterback, Palm Beach, Florida: Starred at Palm Beach's private Ralph Lauren Academy. Was run over by a polo pony during the off-season, however, and suffered head injuries that made him think he is a cocker spaniel.

His father, a wealthy Eastern industrialist, plans to buy him his own Gucci shop as soon as Norman stops chasing Mercedes 380SLs down Worth Avenue.

• *Arnold (Stumpy) Wordsworth,* linebacker, Why-not, Georgia: 6' 3", 290. Got the nickname "Stumpy" from his instructors. Not only did he not answer any questions correctly on his SAT, he ate his pencil. Wants to become air-traffic controller.

• *Gunther Dappleman,* defensive tackle, Shade Tree, Missouri: Stands 7' 3" and weighs 416. Ineligible because of steroid addiction.

• *Alfonidius Johnson,* defensive back, Slick Snake, Florida: Was courted by over 250 schools until it was learned he was given a frog to dissect in biology class and the frog talked him out of it. Plans career wrestling alligators at Crazy Al's reptile farm and discount fireworks.

• *Ramundo Santiago Ornamata Diego Francisco (Earl) Zapata,* soccer-style placekicker, Bogotá, Colombia: Approached by many U.S. schools, turned down all offers, however, to take better paying job in family export business.

- *Sal (Meathead) Monella,* 6'2", 240, linebacker, Thickneck, New Jersey: Currently at Penn State. Prison. Convicted of mail fraud, writing bad checks, and trying to rob a Roto-Rooter van he mistook for a Brink's truck. Plans to become television evangelist after parole.

Recalling My
School Daze

A young woman was expelled from a Goldsboro, North Carolina, high school recently because she modeled a bathing suit in a shopping mall.

A judge later ruled the student, seventeen-year-old Michelle Outlaw, could return to school, however, and justice certainly was served.

High school kids are walking around with green hair, so what's the big deal about modeling a bathing suit?

Kathy Sue Loudermilk, hallowed be her name, entered a Miss Collard Festival beauty pageant back home one year and wore a bathing suit that was much too small to hold everything Kathy Sue had attempted to stuff into it.

During the talent portion of the contest, Kathy Sue was doing her famous "Dueling Kazoos" number, and her suit gave way and split right down the front.

Parents attempted to cover their children's eyes, and the Baptist minister had to be revived with cold water.

Said my boyhood friend and idol, Weyman C. Wannamaker, Jr., a great American, who witnessed the incident, "What kazoos!"

I can't imagine a student being expelled from school for simply modeling a swimsuit. Students were expelled back when I was in high school for sure, but you had to do some heavy-duty rotten stuff to get the gate.

Weyman was expelled for one of the classics of teenage vandalism. He put cherry bombs down each of the three commodes in the boys' room and then flushed.

By some method I'm not certain of, cherry bombs will explode underwater. Not only was the boys' room completely flooded, but they found pieces of broken commode all the way down at the tether-ball pole on the playground.

Weyman's father, Mr. Wannamaker, of Wannamaker Plumbing, gave the school a 10 percent discount on what he charged for cleaning up the mess. It was considered a fine gesture.

Frankie Garfield, the school bully, usually was expelled once a week. Among other things, he once set fire to the school library in an effort to get out of having to read *Les Misérables.* The book was damaged, however. And rumor had it Frankie actually read four pages before his dog, Killer, ate the book.

Frankie also stole a pig and brought it to school in a sack. He set the pig free in the home ec. lab where the students were learning to fry bacon. Three of the girls, thinking the pig was bent on revenge, fainted.

Frankie got expelled, but the pig fared even worse. It ate a sponge cake the home ec. class had prepared, got sick, and died.

Back to Kathy Sue: She fared a lot better than Michelle Outlaw, too. Not only was she not expelled, a ceremony was held and what was left of Kathy Sue's swimsuit was placed on display at the local feed store, which sponsored the Miss Collard Festival pageant.

I guess we were just a lot more liberal back then.

It's Only
Sheepskin Deep

Everyone worries about how much it costs to go to college.

I read a figure that said the cost of one year of schooling at prestigious institutions such as Yale and Harvard and other places, where the football teams never go to a bowl game, was twenty thousand dollars.

One female student interviewed on the Yale campus said, "I think it's worth it."

A Porsche is worth it at fifty thousand dollars, too, if Daddy's check is coming in each month.

It's been twenty years since I was in college, but I still feel I am qualified to offer a few suggestions to parents as to how to cut down on the price of educating their little spoiled darlings.

If you can't finance twenty thousand dollars a year on what you make in annual salary down at the plant, and your kid wants to go to Harvard because that's the best place to go if you want to meet, and perhaps later marry, a Kennedy, suggest alternatives.

"How about good ol' State U?" you might ask.

Your kid's eyes will roll back in his or her head, the classic teenage expression that means you have been completely out of touch with what's happening since the year Rome was sacked.

Then say, "Okay, I can't afford Harvard and you don't want to go to State U, but I can get you on the third shift at the plant." That should work. You wouldn't want your kid to meet and marry a Kennedy anyway. Those people probably wear ties at dinner.

Speaking of work, here's another way to cut down on what it costs to put your child through college.

Suggest he or she get a part-time job to help pay for some of the expenses. This suggestion likely will send your child into a fainting spell.

"But how," your daughter will ask, when she is revived, "can I work and still have time to be on the Homecoming Float Committee at the sorority house?"

Explain how you had to sell magazines door-to-door to put yourself through college, and if she doesn't get a job, there won't be enough money for sorority dues.

Your daughter will hate you, but only until her own children reach college age.

Here are some other ideas of how to cut the high cost of college:

1. Never send your children off to school with a convertible sports car or a credit card. The sports car will break down, and you will have to pay for it to be repaired.

A college-age individual with a credit card will wear the writing off the plastic before Christmas break.

2. Don't allow your child to do anything because one of his or her friends is doing it—you sell used cars, the friend's dad is a television evangelist.

3. As soon as your child leaves for college, move to a new address and get an unlisted phone number so you won't be getting any letters or phone calls begging for money.

Some of these suggestions may seem cruel, but it's either use them or wind up spending a fortune on your kid's education and have him or her marry a Kennedy and when they come over for dinner you won't be able to eat in your shorts.

It's your decision.

Today's Teenage "Slanguage"

Have you listened closely to the way young people talk today?

There are some drastic differences between the way they talk and the way the rest of us talk.

If you have children, you certainly will recognize my first example: Many young people today insist upon using the verb "goes" for verbs like "says," "remarks," "suggests," and "interrupts."

A sixteen-year-old girl in a discussion regarding what happened at school today:

". . . And Poopsie goes, 'I've got tickets to the Nasty Navels concert,' and Tami goes, 'I don't care,' and Poopsie goes, 'You're just mad 'cause you don't have any,' and Tami goes, 'I've got ballet that night, anyway,' and Poopsie goes, 'Shawn is taking me to the concert,' and Tami goes, 'You'll make a lovely couple, you both wear the same kind of earrings.' "

I suppose this is derived from usage of the word "went" to

indicate an utterance or making a sound, as in "ding-ding-ding *went* the trolley."

Kids never use "went," however, and throw tense to the wind with their "goes."

A sixteen-year-old girl discussing what happened several days later at school:

"Poopsie goes, 'Shawn and I had a great time at the Nasty Navels concert,' and I go, 'I don't care,' and Poopsie goes, 'You're just jealous 'cause you didn't get to go,' and I go, 'The Nasty Navels and Shawn both make me want to puke,' and Poopsie goes, 'Your mother certainly dresses you funny,' and I go, 'Do your zits glow in the dark?' "

"Okay" is another word kids use a lot today, and they primarily use it as professional athletes use the phrase "you know"—as a stalling tactic while they think of what it is they want to say next.

There is also the phrase "I'm like," which, if I have listened correctly, translates roughly as "I reacted thusly, or I was in the following state of mind."

A sixteen-year-old girl talking about what happened several weeks after the Nasty Navels concert:

"Tami goes, 'Did you hear about Poopsie?' . . . Okay, and I'm like, 'I can't stand it' . . . Okay, and Tami goes, 'She's pregnant' . . . Okay, and I'm like, 'I don't believe it' . . . Okay, and then Tami goes, 'I think it was Shawn' . . . Okay, and I'm like, 'Give me a break' . . . Okay.

"And Tami goes, 'Her parents are sending her to a home, . . . Okay, and I'm like, 'Ohhhhhh, God!' . . . Okay, and Tami goes, 'Remember how Poopsie didn't pay attention and always painted her nails in sex-ed class?' "

I'm not saying the way young people talk today is necessarily wrong. Lest we forget, each generation has its own eccentricities when it comes to language. Our parents said things like "Twenty-three skidoo" and used "swell" to mean "terrific."

My generation was always "into" disco, yoga, or open marriages.

As it turned out, incidentally, Poopsie wasn't pregnant after all. And Shawn turned out to be gay and is currently a drummer with the Nasty Navels.

Both Poopsie and Shawn wear a lot of Spandex and are into watching *Geraldo.*

Okay?

Capital Punishment

You no doubt heard the bad news that a survey revealed America's youth doesn't know diddly about geography.

I was watching television and there was a follow-up to the survey in which a reporter asked some kid in New York City how many people he thought lived in the entire United States.

He answered, "Like, you know, about a million and a half."

There were a million and a half people trying to cross the street in front of this brain-dead bozo.

But kids aren't the only ones who don't know anything about geography, and I'm not talking about being able to locate the Caspian Sea.

There are adult human beings in this country who can't name five state capitals outside their own state.

The reason I know this is I am probably the greatest living expert on state capitals, and for years I have been amazed how many otherwise intelligent people think St. Louis is the capital of Missouri.

The reason I am probably the world's greatest living expert

on state capitals is because my parents gave me one of those United States map puzzles when I was six. I didn't get what I wanted—a pony—so all I did all year was mess with this puzzle.

I don't care where you went to school or how much money you've made or how much your wife is involved in the Junior League. If you think St. Louis is the capital of Missouri (unless you're a Missourian, of course), you are a geographic bimbo.

Many have tried and many have failed to stump me on a state-capital question. It's like trying to stump Isaac Newton on gravity.

Think you know state capitals? Okay, a little test. Grade yourself honestly:

1. The capital of Florida? You thought it was Orlando? It probably would make sense to have the capital of Florida in Orlando, but it's in Tallahassee.
2. The capital of Illinois? Chicago makes sense, but it's Springfield.
3. California? No, it's Sacramento. The paper there is called the *Bee*.
4. Washington? Not the one on the Potomac, the one where apples come from. Olympia. It's also the name of the local beer.
5. Oregon? Salem.
6. Kentucky? Frankfort, and they don't hold the Derby there.
7. South Dakota? Pierre. I once met a man from Pierre, South Dakota. He said he bowled a lot to pass the time.
8. North Dakota? Bismarck.
9. Montana? I have an ex-wife who lives there. I got ex-wives living everywhere. Helena is the capital of Montana.
10. Nevada? They don't have time for much of the state's business in Las Vegas. The capital is Carson City.

11. New York? You really didn't say New York City, did you? How embarrassing. It's Albany, where Mario Cuomo lives.
12. Four American state capitals begin with the same letter as their state. Can you name them?

Was your first answer Philadelphia, Pennsylvania? Harrisburg is the capital of Pennsylvania, dummy.

The correct answers are: Oklahoma City, Oklahoma; Indianapolis, Indiana; Dover, Delaware; and Honolulu, Hawaii.

As far as Missouri is concerned, if you don't know the state capital, it's your duty as an American to go somewhere and find out.

I'll expect your answers in a week.

Attention, All You Racist, Sexist Swine

There has been a great deal of discussion recently concerning the fairness of the Scholastic Aptitude Test (SAT), which is used to determine how many smarts young people have.

Studies have indicated white males do better on the test than other groups, indicating bias.

So what are we going to do about that?

Are we just going to sit back and say, "Well, I guess that just means white males are smarter than everybody else?"

Of course not. That would make us racist, sexist swine who

probably go to see movies like *The Last Temptation of Christ* and aren't offended by it.

What we need to do about all this is quite clear to me. Why somebody doesn't do well on a test is because he or she doesn't know the answers to certain questions.

The way to get around that is to ask each individual only those questions he or she knows the answers to.

That way, everybody—regardless of age, race, sex, religious affiliation, or hat size—would make a perfect score every time, thus virtually wiping out racism and sexism as we know it today.

The new testing system would work like this:

Each individual test-taker would meet first with a test-monitor. To assure any further bias, the monitor would be of the same sex, race, etc., of that individual.

Together they would go over the test. The questions the individual didn't know the answers to would be thrown out in the spirit of fairness, equality, and keeping hope alive.

After the individual finished his or her (or its) test, the monitor would grade it and then smile and say, "Congratulations, Arlene (Jesse, Juan, Running Buffalo, Chang, Conchita), you have taken the test and you have aced that sucker!"

These individuals could then go on to the college or university of their choice and become rocket scientists.

The only remaining question here is what do we do about the white males who've been hogging all the good grades on the SAT exams?

Although I'm a white male myself, I still think we should be made to pay a price for having the test geared to us all these years.

We should have no pretest interview. We should not have the questions we don't know the answers to thrown out.

We should still have to struggle and sweat over questions about cosines and logarithms.

We should still be made queasy and unsure about answering

such questions as "What is the capital of Denmark?" Is it Copenhagen or Seattle?

And we should have a difficult time getting into the colleges and universities of our choice because everybody else will have perfect grades on their SATs and there we'll be back in the 1200s.

And since all the rocket-scientist jobs will be taken, I guess the only thing left for us to do is join the National Guard.

Is School Lunch Fare Fair?

There's a report out from something called the "Public Voice of Food & Health" (PVF&H) that says school lunches are too high in fat, sugar, and salt.

The report specifically criticizes the U.S. Department of Agriculture, according to news stories I read, for the high fat surplus food it provides the public-school lunch program.

"We'd like to see more schools serve healthfully modified lunches that are still attractive to school children like spaghetti with meatballs or baked potatos with chili," said Eileen Kugler, spokeslady for the PVF&H.

What I want to know is, where was Eileen Kugler and the public voice for whatever it is when I was in school?

Every school day for four years, I had to eat lunch in the high school cafeteria. I don't know about all that high fat and too much salt and sugar business, but I do know somebody was trying to poison me with that food and eventually would have had I not graduated.

I would have loved spaghetti and meatballs and chili with a baked potato.

Perhaps that was part of the problem. If I could have identified what I was being served for lunch, it might have been easier to get it down.

It's tough to look at a plate of food and know only there's some brown stuff, green stuff, and yellow stuff. Maybe the brown stuff was roast beef, perhaps the green was some sort of vegetable, and the yellow a fruit.

Then again, the brown could have come from a camel or a goat, the green could have been something that started out white before it began to mold, and the yellow could have been something imported to this country as a governmental effort to boost a Third World economy.

Occasionally, of course, I would be able to identify something on my plate, but I don't know whether it's worse to be eating government-surplus pickled okra and know it, or be eating government-surplus pickled okra and think it might be something that grows only in a cave.

As far as today's school lunches are concerned, we must remember the children of today are the leaders of tomorrow. Certainly they should not be served food with too much fat or salt or sugar, but they also shouldn't be forced to go through a daily visit to cafeteria-from-hell like we did.

Here is how I would run today's school-lunch program:

1. Each serving should be truthfully identified. Perhaps the boys in shop could make little signs the cooks could stick in the food.
2. Faculty members, as well as lunchroom personnel, should be made to eat the same food the students are being served in full view of the students.

3. Any student requesting seconds should be sent away for psychiatric review.

I recall the immortal words of my boyhood friend and idol, Weyman C. Wannamaker, Jr., a great American. He forked the mystery meat on his plate one day at lunch, held it aloft to study it, and then said, "You'd have to be crazy to eat something as ugly as this."

Today's Teens Discover a New Hangout

A lady, obviously quite distraught, wrote me a letter recently asking that I "write something about all these teenagers sitting on the hoods of their cars at the shopping mall.

"They just sit there at night and play their car radios loud when they should be home," the lady continued.

The lady's name isn't important here. She was writing from Tampa, Florida, but that's not important here.

What is important is that I do, in fact, write something about teenagers sitting on the hoods of their cars at shopping malls, which occurs, I suppose, all over the country.

I think it's a great idea, and I don't know why my generation didn't think of it.

What we did when I was a teenager was drive around the Dairy Queen.

I don't mean we drove around the Dairy Queen once and then drove somewhere else. I mean we drove around and around and around the Dairy Queen, and I'm still not sure why.

It wasn't to locate any of our friends so we could converse with them. They were driving around and around and around the Dairy Queen, too.

It seems that once during all those years, somebody would have had the good sense to ask, "Hey, guys. What are we doing driving around the Dairy Queen? I'm getting nauseous."

But nobody ever said that, so here we would go, burning up no telling how many gallons of gasoline.

During the oil crunch of the seventies, I thought of all the gasoline we wasted as teenagers driving around the Dairy Queen and figured we probably were the ones who at least started the ball rolling toward an oil crisis.

Teenagers are going to hang out somewhere. In biblical days, they probably hung out over where the goats were being watered. The problem there was all the flies.

In the Old West, they hung out over at the livery stable. Me, I hate liver, but I didn't grow up in the Old West.

Our parents hung out down at the corner store eating penny candy on their six-mile walk home from school.

I say, let today's teenagers hang out sitting on the hoods of their cars at shopping malls if they want to.

Think of the precious gasoline that is being preserved, and as long as teenagers are sitting on the hoods of their cars, they aren't going to be out terrorizing the roads and highways.

It is basically impossible to terrorize on a road or a highway while sitting on the hood of your car at a shopping mall.

I do admit young people have a tendency to turn up the sound on their car radios as far as it will go.

What I do when I am confronted by a young person playing

loud music on his or her car radio is drive as far away from them as I can.

Which is what the lady who wrote from Tampa should do. Drive far away and let the kids enjoy being young so they won't grow up to be old goats like her.

10

ON THE ROAD

Caught Short in Bermuda

Hamilton, Bermuda, is paradise. The water is blue as the sky and the temperature is perfect. Spring has colored the island with its glorious reds, pinks, yellows, and whites and people sit on ocean overlooks and sip drinks made stout with rum.

I should be thankful a bit of business has landed me here.

I'm not, however. I usually can get along with just about everybody, even liberal Democrats and chiropractors, but I am having a difficult time dealing with Bermudans.

You've heard about it in Jamaica, and maybe you've experienced it in the Bahamas. Add Bermuda to the list.

Many of the locals, most of whom make their living off the tourist trade, have no use for tourists.

I'm supposed to play golf at the Mid-Ocean Club. Very British. Lots of portraits of scowling old men on the walls. I walked into the starter's office.

"Hello," I began. "I'm supposed to play golf with . . ."

"You're not playing golf here in those shorts," the starter interrupted me.

"What's wrong with my shorts?" I asked.

"Too short," said the starter. "Don't you tourists know anything?"

To avoid an ugly scene, I went to the pro shop and bought

shorts with the proper length. They were quite ugly and cost me forty bucks.

Back to the starter. A companion had joined me.

"I'd like to have two carts," he said to Mr. Sunshine.

"You don't tell me what you want to have," the starter snapped. "I tell you what I will allow you to have."

We got even. Neither of us replaced our divots during our golf round. I can make divots—holes in the ground—in which a small boy could get lost.

Cab drivers. One berates our group because we try to get into his cab bearing cups.

"You're not getting into my cab with those cups," he says with the distinct aroma of admonishment. "You might spill something on my seats."

"Forget it, Heloise," I said, "we'll walk."

Walking in Bermuda is dangerous. They drive on the wrong side of the road, for one thing, and if you are a Bermudan and you run over a tourist, you get a free ticket to the cricket matches or some other valuable premium.

The night doorman at the front of the Sonesta Beach Hotel. I walk out and say, "Taxi."

"You don't say 'taxi,'" he spits at me. "I say 'taxi.'"

I'm stupid enough to argue with the guy, and he says he'll have me put in the "jug"—Bermudan for jail.

He never did tell me what the charge would be. Saying "taxi" when it wasn't my turn, I suppose.

I'm leaving Bermuda today. When my flight is safely airborne, I am going to turn back and give Bermuda a well-known gesture.

The beauty here just ain't worth the bother.

Back to Paradise

A few months ago, I visited Bermuda and did not have a very good time.

A starter at a local private golf course made some rather crude remarks concerning my shorts being too short, I got into a shouting match with a hotel doorman because I called to a taxi without consulting him first, and a hotel bartender threatened to punch me out when I mentioned fifteen minutes was a long time to wait for a drink.

I wrote in Hamilton about my bad experiences and received mixed reactions.

Several readers wrote to tell me how they also have been treated rudely in Bermuda.

Others, including the Bermuda tourist agency, suggested I be thrashed by irate cricket players for my remarks.

The Hamilton newspaper even ran a story and headlined it NEGATIVE WRITER RETURNS TO ISLAND—which is the subject for today's effort.

I have indeed returned to Bermuda to make a speech, for which I shall receive a check.

Otherwise, I wouldn't have returned to Bermuda.

I wasn't sure what to expect, so I got off my plane at the Bermuda airport dressed in a disguise. I wore socks.

I got to my hotel, the Southampton Princess, without incident. I checked into my room and bolted the door and remained there until the next morning.

It was then I ventured out of my room for the first time and went down for breakfast, which was no longer being served.

I asked for lunch.

"Lunch isn't served until eleven-thirty," I was told.

"Then, I'll just have a Coke," I said.

"No Coke," I was told. "The bar doesn't open until eleven."

I went into a news shop to buy a paper.

"All we have are yesterday's papers," the clerk said.

"When do today's papers come in?" I asked.

"Late tomorrow," was the answer.

I went back to my room.

Later, I ventured out again to play golf. This time I went to a public course and nobody made fun of the way I was dressed, except my playing partners, who thought my shorts, which came to just above my ankles, were overdoing it a bit.

The next morning, after breakfast, there wasn't any coffee on my table, but I spotted a pot on a nearby counter.

I attempted to pour myself a cup, but a waiter snatched the pot away from me and told me to sit down, he'd bring me the coffee.

I did, and he did, and in a few hours I'll be on a plane out of here.

In conclusion, may I say I have not experienced half the hassles in Bermuda as I experienced before, and that may or may not be directly related to the fact I have spent a lot of time in my room, have never complained about a single thing, and have sat down and shut up whenever anybody told me to.

Had I had the same attitude any of the three times I've been married, one of them just might have worked out.

Into the Woods—
to Go Camping

My good friend Browny Stephens is an expert camper.

He knows where all those poles and stakes that come with tents actually go, and he can put up a tent in less than fifteen minutes.

He puts his salt and pepper and coffee in little containers that are easily packed, he can eat freeze-dried grits for breakfast with no apparent problem, and the zipper on his sleeping bag never gets stuck.

He's also hiked long portions of the Appalachian Trail.

"Can you take a dog with you on the Trail?" I asked him.

"Not where there are any bears," he said. "Dogs attract bears."

I know very little about camping. As a matter of fact, I am a camping disaster.

I attract bugs and rain. I injure myself and others while attempting to erect a tent, and when I was in the Boy Scouts, the zipper of my sleeping bag got stuck with me in it.

The scoutmaster had to call Shorty's Texaco to bring over various tools with which they cut me out of my sleeping bag.

Regardless of all this, however, Browny took me camping with him during my recent vacation. He is a kind and patient man. We went camping somewhere in the woods of North Carolina.

"The drought has been terrible here," he said, as he put up my tent. "They haven't had rain in weeks."

A half hour later, it rained and put out our fire before the hamburgers had time to cook thoroughly.

"If you can't eat raw hamburger," Browny said, "I can fix you up with some freeze-dried grits."

I found a box of raisins in Browny's pack and ate them.

It rained the second night, too.

Desperate, I put some raisins in my freeze-dried grits. As I was eating, a large bug flew into my bowl. I don't know if it was the collision that killed the bug or the freeze-dried grits.

The third night was the night of the skunk.

"Lots of skunks around here," the forest ranger had warned us.

I asked Browny, "What do you do if you see a skunk wandering into your campsite?"

"The most important thing," he explained, "is not to frighten the skunk. Be very still and let the skunk have whatever it is looking for. Losing a little food is a lot better than being sprayed by a skunk."

It was just about time to crawl into my tent, when I saw the skunk.

He came out from behind a tree and seemed to be headed directly toward our campsite.

"Skunk!" I screamed. "There's a skunk coming toward us!"

"See how fast that skunk ran after I screamed at it?" I asked Browny later.

"Would you hang around a place that smelled this bad?" he asked back.

Other than all of that, we had a great camping trip, which is to say I didn't poke out anybody's eye with a tentpole, or leave the lighter-fluid can too near the fire and cause an explosion.

I felt so confident after our trip, I mentioned to Browny I

might want to tackle the Appalachian Trail one of these days.

"I've got to be in Czechoslovakia that week," he said, "but maybe you can take along your dog."

Cabin Fever at 21 Below

I met a man from South Dakota on the golf course in Orlando the other day. What I'm doing in Orlando is covering the warm weather for all those other poor souls stuck in the ravages of winter.

What I wanted to know from the man from South Dakota was, "What are you doing here?"

"What do you mean, what am I doing here?" he asked back. "When I left South Dakota it was twenty-one below. That's what I'm doing here."

The guy's name was Roger. The temperature that surrounded us was 83.

Before I met Roger, I had never met anybody from South Dakota. There even have been times when I've had serious doubts whether or not there actually is a South Dakota.

I know there's not a North Dakota. What you think is North Dakota is actually part of Canada, and it's so cold and bleak there the Canadians are trying to pass it off as a part of this country. Acid rain is how we're getting even.

"What's it like," I asked Roger, "when it's twenty-one below?"

"When you go outside," he said, "if the wind don't get you,

the frostbite will. If you stay inside, you soon will develop cabin fever and begin chasing your loved ones around with an ax. That's why I came here. One more day in that house, and I'd have to do a Jack Nicholson."

Jack Nicholson got cabin fever in a movie and chased his loved ones around with an ax. He should have come to Florida and worked out his frustrations on the golf course.

"Roger," I asked, "are you ever going back to South Dakota?"

"Sooner or later," he said.

"Roger," I went on, "let me explain something to you. There are at least forty-seven other states that have weather better than South Dakota.

"I suppose South Dakota has better weather than Alaska and North Dakota, but that's about it.

"Even Nebraska and Iowa have better weather than South Dakota. It gets cold in Maine, but the lobster is cheap and maybe you can get a glimpse of President Bush.

"Think about southern California, Roger. It snowed there the other day, but it was a mistake. The Dodgers are in southern California, and so is the San Diego Zoo. And getting it in an earthquake would at least be quicker than taking two or three days to freeze to death.

"Listen, Roger," I continued, "there's also Arizona. You'd never have sinus problems in Arizona.

"And Kentucky and Tennessee are beautiful and Georgia is gorgeous. And there are the lovely Carolinas and Virginia is for lovers, and if you throw out the city, New York is even a nice state.

"And think about Florida, Roger. If you lived in Florida, you could have great weather all year. Sure, Florida has its problems with tourists and drug dealers, but you could live with that.

"What I'm saying to you, Roger," I went on, coming to the climax of my remarks, "is I want to feel sorry for you and your family and the freezing people of South Dakota, but I can't.

Aren't there buses and airplanes that leave South Dakota?

"Of course there are. Go home and get your family, Roger, and get the hell out of South Dakota."

Roger seemed genuinely impressed with what I said, and if I convince just one family to move out of places like South Dakota before they freeze or start chopping one another up with axes, I feel I would have done a great service to mankind.

In Lieu of That Swimsuit Issue

Sports Illustrated's annual swimsuit issue, as the magazine's writers explained about 195 times, is an attempt to make February *bareable* to its readers.

February is the worst month of the year in most portions of the country. It's damp and cold in February, and football is over and baseball hasn't started yet and basketball and hockey still have an eternity to go.

So *Sports Illustrated* puts out an issue filled with photographs of pretty girls in swimsuits. Or, as the years and swimsuit issues have gone by, photographs of pretty girls in skimpy swimsuits.

As we hurtle toward the 1990's, it is now possible to buy a copy of *Sports Illustrated* and see a pair of women's breasts. I knew when the American League adopted the designated hitter rule, sports would never be the same.

But enough about *Sports Illustrated,* and let's get on with what I'm doing in Orlando.

Hey, *Sports Illustrated* doesn't own the idea to give its readers something to get by on during February.

I simply looked at a color weather map in the paper the other day and noticed it was mostly white and blue all over the country.

For those who don't look at color newspaper maps, if it's white where you live, dare not walk outside lest your nose hairs freeze.

If it's blue where you live, it's not that much better. About the only place on the weather map where it was orange—which means it's nice and warm and your nose hairs stand no chance of freezing—was Florida.

So I said to myself, "Why don't I go to Florida and write about the niceness and the warmness so people who read my report will feel better about the fact they're stuck in various Siberias with frozen nose hairs?"

I chose Orlando because I'm afraid to go to Miami. That's not the only reason. Orlando is a vibrant city with ideal weather, lots of great golf courses, and I have a friend here who knows the owner of the city's best steakhouse and can get us a table without having to go through the usual one-hour wait.

So, it reached a high of 83 the first day I arrived in Orlando. There were no clouds. Not one.

I checked into the Grand Cypress Hyatt Regency. The next morning I went down to the pool and had my coffee and read the paper while getting a bit of sun.

It was nice and warm down by the pool.

After lunch I went over to the golf course and played eighteen holes.

It was nice and warm over at the golf course.

I didn't have a good front nine. I had trouble adjusting to the fact I wasn't wearing a hat, two sweaters, and long underwear.

But at the turn, I bought myself a tall cold drink and sat out on the patio, and by that time I was getting used to the fact I was actually playing golf in a pair of shorts.

I shot 40 on the back. I parred ten, eleven, and twelve and then double-bogeyed at thirteen. I parred fourteen, fifteen, and sixteen. Then, I bogeyed seventeen and eighteen.

Afterward, I bought myself another tall cold drink and went back to the patio and watched the golden sunset.

It was nice and warm out on the patio.

The forecast is for more good weather in Orlando. I plan more mornings down by the pool, more golf, and more drinks out on the patio.

Some people might ask, "Isn't he really doing this because he wants those of us who can't just pick up and go chase the sun to feel jealous?"

I promise I'm not. I'm doing this for you. I swear on my toasty nose hairs.

Back-Home Thoughts

What is wrong with too many of us is we never get to spend any time in places like Palatka, Florida, anymore.

I'm not saying I'm ready to pack it up and move to Palatka right now, but I spent a couple of days there recently, and I'm better off for it.

Palatka has a population of about twelve thousand. It sits on the banks of the St. Johns River, wide and blue, sixty miles south of Jacksonville.

There's a paper mill and a furniture factory.

I made a speech in a place that is a country and western juke joint on the weekends.

"Not much to do in Palatka," a man apologized to me.

I wouldn't say that. Country star John Conlee was due in the juke joint soon, and Palatka calls itself the bass-fishing capital of the world.

Unless you've been to a country juke joint on a Saturday night or bass-fished with somebody who knows where the glory holes are, your life is miserably incomplete.

There's a Holiday Inn in Palatka. It has one of those satellite dishes that enables first-run movies to be shown in the rooms for a price. I stayed in the Holiday Inn and ordered a Nick Nolte movie called *Weeds.* Next to *Kiss of the Spider Woman,* it was the worst movie I'd ever seen.

But that's the only bad thing that happened to me in Palatka.

My first morning, I went to the Holiday Inn restaurant and ordered my eggs the same way I always order them: "over medium well."

That means the yellow doesn't run out of the egg, it merely *crawls.*

Rarely do I ever get my eggs cooked correctly. In Palatka I did. Plus, when the waitress served my eggs, she smiled and said, "If these aren't cooked the way you like them, just tell me and I'll get 'em done over for you."

There is a place in heaven for smiling, cooperative waitresses.

I played golf in Palatka at the municipal course, the only one in town. It was packed.

"It's the Yankees," a local explained to me. "They come down this time of year. We get the poor ones. The rich ones go on down to Ft. Lauderdale or Palm Beach."

The course was charming. So was my partner, who at one point in the match made five straight birdies.

"They take golf real seriously in Palatka," the pro was saying.

Perhaps it was the sunshine that got to me. It was the first time I'd had off from winter for a while.

Or maybe it was the people I met. There was a warmth to them, too. Throw in the eggs and the smiling waitress and how gorgeous the river looked in the morning, and I started getting all those back-home thoughts again.

So many of us sprang from origins like Palatka, only to be gobbled by the urban monster.

But you can go back. And I will someday. To my Palatka.

I'm not certain where that is just yet, but the thing is, I've started looking. For that, I thank Palatka.

11

SPORTS

Ol' Granny's Curse

Homer Dawson of Atlanta has written me an intriguing letter, complete with information why the local teams who perform in Atlanta Stadium—the Braves and the Falcons—have been lousy since the day the stadium was erected.

Mr. Dawson, who describes himself as an "elderly Atlantan," has had his secret for many years, but now that there is talk of building a new stadium, he wrote, he feels it is time to come forward with his story.

"I swore an oath many years ago that I wouldn't tell nobody this story," Mr. Dawson's letter began.

"But now that they're talking about building a new place to play ball, I have to tell you about 'The Curse of Atlanta Stadium.' "

Please continue, Mr. Dawson:

"Way back in the 60s, when they were going to build the stadium, they had to tear down some old houses. They called it Urban Renewal.

"Well, there was this one old, old lady living in that area. Nobody knew her name. Everybody just called her Ol' Granny.

"Ol' Granny didn't have any place to move and her house was in the way of the new stadium.

"She fought 'em as hard as she could. She'd been living in the same place for 87 years and she vowed she wouldn't move without a fight.

"Ol' Granny was never going to win this one, though, so before she moved she decided she would do something to fix this new stadium and whoever was going to play ball there.

"Everybody around the area knew Ol' Granny was a part-time witch. One night before they tore her house down, when the moon was full, she went out in her backyard and dug a hole.

"That hole is right where the Atlanta Stadium pitcher's mound is this very day.

"Ol' Granny threw some lizard lips and buzzard feathers in the hole. She put in some rattlesnake hides and possum tails.

"Then, she covered all this up and sprinkled bat whiskers on top of it and wet it down with skunk mist.

"Then, Ol' Granny made her curse. She said, 'Ain't no ball team ever going to be any good that makes this stadium their home.

"There won't ever be anything but failure, and them that runs the teams are going to get fired and as long as they play ball in this backyard, they're gonna be cursed.' "

Ol' Granny moved away before they bulldozed her house and nobody knew whatever became of her.

But her curse? It could be true. What better explanation do we have for both the Braves and Falcons being flops all these hopeless seasons?

Do demons lurk in the dugouts and under the goal posts? Perhaps it is Ol' Granny's curse that has brought Atlanta so many lousy quarterbacks, sore-armed pitchers, and stumblebum coaches, managers, and general managers.

Call in an exorcist. Get Pat Robertson to pray. Get Roto-Rooter involved if necessary.

One more thing from Homer Dawson: "Tell (owner) Rankin Smith if he builds another stadium not to tear down any more witches' houses."

Sound advice. Skunk mist, huh? I always thought it was the quality of play that made the stadium smell so bad.

My Most
Valuable Players

I was having an impromptu interview with Howard Fox, a member of the executive committee of the Minnesota Twins baseball team, during a Twins spring training game against the world-champion New York Mets, a group of famous millionaires.

Mr. Fox told me something I didn't know. He said the average salary for major-league baseball players today is in excess of $400,000 a year.

That's the *average* salary.

"How do these guys get paid," I asked, "by the week?"

"Twice a month, but just during the season," he answered.

"Do you mail their checks to their banks, or to their agents?" I continued.

"Most of our guys come by and we hand them their checks," said Mr. Fox.

I did some figuring. Let's say a player makes $1 million a year, which a lot of them do, even utility infielders.

He's paid twice weekly for approximately six months, so that means each time he's handed his check his gross is for something around $83,000.

I'm for everybody making all the bucks he or she can, but every time I watch a bunch of spoiled crybaby baseball players, like the Mets, it makes me even more aware of how we need to reward others in our society with a lot more than they are making.

I made a list of some examples:

- *Schoolteachers*   If it weren't for my teachers, I couldn't have figured out the biweekly check for a millionaire ball-player.

    My mother taught first grade for thirty years. The first six months of every year, she worked mostly on house-breaking half her class. She went back to teaching in 1953 after she and my father divorced. She was paid $120 a month. Batboys make more than that.
- *Airline Pilots*   They already make a lot of money, but they also should have a bonus clause that says each time they land one of those tubs safely, they get a few more bucks.

    I want my airline pilots to have a great deal of incentive to get me back on the ground safely.
- *Cops and Firemen*   Next time you're getting mugged or your house is on fire, call your favorite utility in-fielder.
- *Secretaries*   Most executives could not function were it not for their secretaries. Relief pitchers in baseball are paid according to how many "saves" they have.

    Secretaries should be paid on the same basis for the number of times they save their bosses from embarrassing situations, such as being discovered as total incompetents.
- *Garbagemen*   They keep us from being overrun by our own wastefulness, and for a paltry pittance of pay we expect them to take away our garbage at five in the morning and not make any noise.
- *Ministers who don't have their own TV shows*   These are the people who don't make very much money, yet they still console the troubled, visit the sick, and pray for the dead, and don't get to wear any makeup.

Jim Bakker, Jerry Falwell, Jimmy Swaggart, et al., couldn't carry their Bibles.

Think about it. And the next time you need somebody to lean on, call Darryl Strawberry.

Casanova Couldn't Get to First Base

Each spring we come back to West Palm Beach—we are bartenders and lawyers, and salesmen and accountants, and aging columnists.

We come for the sun, while Winter takes its last gasps through the northern parts, and to watch the joy that is spring-training baseball.

We saw our team, the Atlanta Braves, play the Dodgers. The Braves led 3–0 going into the ninth inning, but the Dodgers scored three times and eventually won in the tenth.

Afterward, one of us said, with an unmistakable sadness in his voice, "It's going to be another long year."

If you happen to live in a city where there is winning baseball, be thankful for it.

Baseball has not been very good to Atlanta.

Some of us are single. One, who shall remain nameless, had yet another purpose for making the trip south this year besides sun and baseball.

He came to meet an heiress.

"They're everywhere down here," he was telling me.

"You go over to Palm Beach and hang around on Worth Avenue and you're bound to meet one."

Palm Beach, of course, is one of the best addresses on the continent.

Worth Avenue is where the people who live at this address go to shop and sit in well-appointed restaurants and bars, sipping Dom Perignon, an expensive champagne, not to be confused with the rookie third baseman of the same name.

"I've already been married and divorced twice," my friend explained. "I've gotten the death penalty both times.

"I figure I meet an heiress, get married, and lie around in the sun for the next twenty-five years watching polo matches. I've got it coming to me."

"What sort of heiress do you have in mind?" I asked.

"It really doesn't matter," he answered. "I'll take a Firestone, the daughter of a South American wealthy coffee magnate, even a fat girl with glasses whose daddy made a fortune in trucking."

He dressed for the evening, resplendent in Polo and Gucci. I wished him luck.

He was late to the ball game in Vero Beach the next day. The Braves were playing the Dodgers again.

"So," I asked, "how did you do?"

"Pay dirt," he beamed. "She's tall, and has a New England accent. I figure old money.

"She gave me her number. I'm going to call her after the seventh inning."

The Dodgers got four in the first, but the Braves later took the lead.

Casanova came back from his phone call and I could see the disappointment in his face.

"Bad news?"

"The number she gave me," he said, "was for the time and temperature."

The Dodgers came back to beat the Braves again. My friend fell silent during the drive back to West Palm.

I told him what Braves fans have learned to say in such similar moments of bitter disappointment.

There's always next year.

Why I Hate the Yankees

One of the reasons I am always happy when baseball season begins is that I have a target at which to aim my hatred, thus simplifying my life.

The games are on, and it's time to start hating the New York Yankees again.

I don't think anybody really likes the Yankees, not even the Yankees themselves. I think some people say they are Yankee fans only as a means of getting attention.

I hate these people, too, and I hope they get constipated.

The good news is, I have just obtained a copy of *The Official New York Yankees Haters' Handbook.* It is not a new book, but it can still be purchased ($5.95, Perigee Books).

It was written by William B. Mead, an Orioles fan, who gets directly to the point in his introduction.

"We hate the Yankees," he writes, "for many reasons. They're spoiled rotten. They think they're such Hot Stuff. Their owner is obnoxious. They pout, sulk and whine, no matter how much they are paid and pampered. Their fans are gross and crude."

Mr. Mead takes you throughout Yankee history, and if you didn't already hate the Yankees before reading the book, you certainly would upon completing it.

Hereby, a list of wonderful reasons from the *Handbook* to hate anybody wearing pinstripes:

- Yogi Berra said very few of those witty things he was supposed to have said. Mead quotes Bill Veeck: "Yogi is a completely manufactured product."

  Berra's teammates called him "the Ape."
- The Yankee players despised Casey Stengel. "Stengel," writes Mead, "charmed sportswriters, but to his players, he was grumpy and intolerable."
- Marilyn Monroe left Joe DiMaggio after nine months of marriage, giving the following reason: "All he wanted to do was watch television."
- The very day Don Larsen pitched his perfect game in the World Series, his wife filed for divorce.
- As newlyweds, Mantle and Billy Martin lived in adjoining apartments, and they occasionally peeked into the other's bedroom window to watch the sexual action.
- Yankee owner George Steinbrenner dismissed his biographer, saying he wanted to write his own life story as an inspiration to American youth.
- The Baby Ruth candy bar wasn't named after Babe Ruth. It was named for President Grover Cleveland's daughter, Ruth.
- Ruth was contemptuous of Lou Gehrig. Said Ruth's daughter, "The Ruths don't speak to the Gehrigs."
- Ruth would wave his paycheck at the other Yankee players and taunt them about their meager pay. Reggie Jackson, meanwhile, enjoyed pulling out rolls of hundred-dollar bills and counting them in public.

And just in case anybody ever begins to feel guilty about hating the Yankees, Mead also quotes Mike Royko of Chicago, my favorite columnist, with this line:

"Hating the Yankees is as American as pizza pie, unwed mothers, and cheating on your income tax."

Little Eddie, R.I.P.

Each time I read another article about baseball pitchers scuffing the balls (which allegedly makes them curve and dip and stuff like that) I think of Little Eddie Estes.

I grew up practically next door to Eddie and his family. He was a couple of years younger than I was, but we shared a common passion—baseball.

The Baptist church sponsored a baseball team in my home-town. This wasn't official Little League. This was blue jeans and T-shirts and lending your glove to somebody on the other team when you went to bat.

Eddie was ten when he joined the team as its youngest member. Eddie eventually would become the best twelve-year-old center fielder I ever saw, but at ten he was small and punchless at bat and needed much work on his defense.

So for two years, our coach played Eddie at "bird dog," a position even the most ardent baseball fans likely are not familiar with.

I'll explain.

Our team had a severe scarcity of baseballs. We got two or three at the beginning of the season and that was that.

A few feet behind home plate at the elementary school

ballfield where we played was a dog pen, home for two rather rowdy bird dogs.

When a foul ball was hit into the pen, which occurred quite often, the dogs immediately launched a frantic effort to retrieve it and have at it with their teeth.

Somebody had to stay in the dog pen at all times in order to get the foul balls before the dogs did, so the game, and the season, could continue.

That position became known as "bird dog."

That somebody who played it was poor little Eddie, who spent two seasons battling the dogs for the precious horsehide.

You play the same balls all season, ones that large dogs are trying their best to destroy, you know something about scuffing.

This story has a happy ending, and then a sad one.

Little Eddie, as I mentioned before, became a gifted center fielder and a big RBI man.

He developed speed and he developed power, and after spending two years fighting off two dogs for foul balls, running down line drives was nothing to him.

He made one of the greatest catches I've ever seen in a game against Mills Chapel, then turned and threw out the tying run at the plate and got his name mentioned in the weekly paper.

(I was our team's correspondent and I compared the catch to Willie Mays's grab on Vic Wertz back whenever that was.)

I think little Eddie was fourteen when he got killed. The car rounded a curve and the driver lost control. I was a pallbearer. I still see his mother occasionally when I get home to visit the folks.

This was supposed to be about scuffing baseballs, but I got off track.

Excuse me. I think it was a lump in my throat that did it.

Bike Riders, Beware

Highlights of the recent Tour de France bicycle race were on my television and a companion said, "Look at all those people on bicycles."

There were a lot of them, granted. In fact, it looked like half of Europe was pedaling along.

But I was not impressed.

"You think the Tour de France is something?" I asked. "You ought to see the streets in my neighborhood."

I'm not certain when, how, or why so many adults decided to start riding bicycles again, but each day that I drive, I see more and more of them out on the streets for a pedal. I suppose all this is in the name of exercise.

It was hard enough when you had to dodge joggers. Now, you have to keep one eye out for drunk drivers and another out for a forty-five-year-old man trying to bike his belly off.

The cyclists in my neighborhood are quite smug. If I were riding on a bicycle on a busy street and a car pulled behind me, I would do the sensible thing and pull to one side.

The reason for that is simple. Were a car to run into a bicycle, the car and its driver likely would come out of the collision without a scratch.

The bicycle, on the other hand, would suffer a severe bending and its rider would be lucky to be sitting up taking solid food in six months.

But the cyclists in my neighborhood ignore all that. I drive up behind them and they pretend I'm not there.

It's as if they were saying, "This may look like a busy roadway for automobiles, but it's really a bicycle path and you have no business on it."

Now, I pull up behind cyclists, blow my horn, and then roar

past them, offering a familiar hand message as I go by. It's as if I were saying, "May your privates get caught in your spokes."

There is something else:

Why is it necessary for these overgrown Schwinnsters to wear those bicycling uniforms? When I rode a bicycle—back when I was twelve—I wore blue jeans.

But notice cyclists today. They wear helmets and those tight stretch outfits that do some rather serious clinging.

The other day, I was driving to the store for beer, and I found myself behind a rather large woman riding a bicycle.

Her outfit appeared to have been stretched beyond the wildest of imaginations.

Her behind was so large, as a matter of fact, for a moment it blocked out my view of the sun.

"My God!" I said, quoting a line from an old *Saturday Night Live* script, "it's a rectal eclipse."

There is hope, however. I read recently of a new study that indicates males who wear their trousers too tight can have very low sperm counts as a result, and have a difficult time fathering children.

As tight as those bicycle pants are, there's a good chance this generation of pedalers may be the last.

For Sale: One Complete Ski Outfit

I used to go skiing about this time each year, despite the fact that natives of the Deep South know their way around snow much the same as a rhinoceros knows its way around roller skates.

It used to cost me quite a bit of money to go skiing. After buying ski pants and ski socks and ski jackets and ski sweaters and ski underwear, I still had to buy a plane ticket that would fly me two thousand miles to some expensive ski resort out West.

Then I had to rent skis and boots and buy lift tickets.

All this to have the opportunity to stand atop a mountain in subzero temperatures trembling in fear as I tried to figure out how I could get to the bottom to thaw out without killing or maiming myself, not to mention what might happen to others who came into my path.

It would have been simpler, and cheaper, to have gotten a root canal. I could have had the same amount of fun.

The reason I began skiing in the first place is I am gullible.

My friend said, "Why don't you go skiing with me? You'll love it."

I believed him. I really believed I would go skiing and fall in love with it, and become a great skier and change my name to Lars Earl. (You know how Southerners like double first names.)

I didn't love skiing after I tried it once, but I have continued to ski because I thought it would get easier and more comfortable.

Wrong again. The hassle factor in the sport of skiing never eased for me.

First there were the boots. Ski boots weigh approximately the same as a Honda.

It takes the better part of an hour to get them on because of the number of straps and buckles that have to be fastened.

Walking in a pair of ski boots is another matter. The next time you watch *Cool Hand Luke,* notice how easily the prisoners move with a ball and chain and you will know what it is like to attempt to walk in a pair of ski boots.

Then comes the lift, which is what you ride to the top of the mountain in order to ski back down it.

There is always a long line waiting on the lift. And I always got on with somebody who weighed six hundred pounds and made the lift chair lean dangerously.

Once I tried to get off a lift with a four-hundred-pound ski bunny sitting next to me. She fell during her dismount and landed on top of me.

Big Foot lives.

Skiing can be embarrassing, too. I never fell when I was skiing alone or when I was off on some distant run. I always fell either in the lift line or directly under the lift, so I always had an audience, which inevitably included small children, from places like Utah and Colorado, who would point and laugh at me.

All this to say I'm not going to return to the slopes as usual this winter. As a matter of fact, I'm never going skiing again.

The bother isn't worth it. And snow ain't my style.

Ol' Lars Earl here has hung up his boots for good.

See you where the sun shines.

12

INTERNATIONAL RELATIONS

Why Not Toss a Coin?

A number of things bother me about the Iran–Iraq war.

First, did Iran invade Iraq or did Iraq invade Iran? And is it the Iraq–Iran war, or the Iran–Iraq war? Do we have the basis for rock lyrics here: "Did Iran invade Iraq/or did Iraq invade Iran?/Iraq–Iran, Iran–Iraq/Iraq around the clock/Stay and be my lovin' man."

Second, I never know what to believe when I read about the war.

One day, the headlines read, IRAQ CLAIMS 7 ZILLION IRANIANS KILLED IN A DESERT BATTLE.

The next day, I get IRAN SAYS NOBODY LEFT IN IRAQ BUT DOGS AND CAMELS.

For all we really know, there might not be a war going on at all. This could be just some public-relations firm's way of introducing a new line of desert tents.

What else bothers me is that I'm not certain who to pull for in the war.

Would the United States benefit more if Iran won, or if Iraq won? How would the war's outcome affect my winter heating bill and gasoline prices? Which side has the best-looking uniforms? (I often use that to determine whom I'd prefer in a sporting contest, which is why I never pull for the Houston Astros, whose uniforms look like they were patterned after a dish of orange marmalade.)

If Iran wipes out a few million Iraqis (Irocks, Iraqanians, Iraqonians), should I sleep a little better at night, or vice versa?

Just off the top of my head, I'd say I should pull for Iraq. The Iranians took Americans hostage; the ayatollah, who looks like Gabby Hayes with a bad case of constipation, has given our last two presidents that same condition; and two of its leading exports are hatred and terrorism. But Iraq's not exactly a bastion of freedom and goodwill to all, either. If Iran is John Dillinger, Iraq is at least Pretty Boy Floyd.

I interviewed some other Americans to see which side they favored.

Tossing out those who hadn't heard about the war, didn't have an opinion, were drunk, who thought I was a member of some strange religious sect, who were busy writing Oral Roberts a check, and who were blowing bubbles with their saliva when they were asked, the results were too close to call.

One man did put the matter in its proper perspective, however.

"It's like asking to pick between cancer and AIDS," he said.

Perhaps what we all have here is the same position the late Georgian Bill Munday, pioneer sportscaster, found himself in one evening before he was to broadcast the Yale–Harvard football game. "Who do you prefer in tomorrow's game?" a Harvard student asked him, "Yale or fair Harvard?"

"Neither one," he said. "You're all a bunch of damn Yankees and I hope you both lose."

The Wall Around the Russians

A couple of years ago, I spent two weeks in the Soviet Union. I thought that experience would enlighten me as to what it is like to be locked out of the rest of the world.

In some ways, it did.

The only news I could get had been tampered with by the government. Guards went through my luggage and took away a football media guide I was carrying as reading material. They thought it had to do with politics, and I wasn't allowed to bring it into the country.

I couldn't get into my hotel unless I showed a guard my pass. Citizens of the Soviet Union are not allowed inside hotels where tourists are staying.

I was warned not to smile when my picture was taken for my visa. I asked why not.

"The Soviets," I was told, "are suspicious of smiles."

But all that gave me only a brief hint of life from behind a wall, a barbed wire fence, a curtain of iron.

All the time I was in the Soviet Union, I knew I would be leaving soon.

Those millions of other poor souls would have to stay.

Something I tried to get answered during those two weeks is why there weren't more protests by Soviet citizens against the tyranny of the government.

Americans wouldn't stand for such a thing, of course. We would march, riot, and die to remove our shackles. We have done it many times before.

I did manage to come away with a few reasons why people of the Soviet Union continue to take whatever the government wants to dish out for them.

- The Soviet people are patriotic. For centuries they have had to guard against invasions of countless hordes and armies. There remain the markings of German shells on buildings in Leningrad where the Soviets held on against the Nazi siege in World War II.
- There is a legacy of oneness and safety in numbers that binds the Soviet masses.
- The Soviet people don't compare their lives to others who live in freedom because they know little of what else is beyond their guarded boundaries and the government wants to keep it that way. How are you going to keep 'em down on the farm, etc.?

We constantly tell ourselves how precious our freedom is, but most of us still take it for granted and I am as guilty as any.

But there is this one thing:

I can tell you when the Lufthansa flight from Moscow to Frankfurt lifted its wheels off Soviet turf, the group of Americans with whom I was traveling broke out into a spontaneous cheer.

Some even cried.

The Russians Out in the Code

I didn't find it all that newsworthy to learn that the Russian and American governments often used bugging devices to find out what one another is doing and/or saying.

I always had taken this as a given. Wasn't the first thing Bill Cosby and Robert Culp did when they checked into a hotel room in *I Spy* was to search out the bugging devices, which always were located in the flowerpot?

I also figure both U.S. and Soviet operatives are smart enough to know how to say things in code when they know they are being listened to by the other side.

My stepbrother, Ludlow Porch of WSB/radio in Atlanta, who happens to be an ex-marine and quite the patriot, was along with me on a trip to the Soviet Union a couple of years ago and we often carried on sensitive conversations in our respective hotel rooms.

We certainly took for granted our rooms were bugged, especially after one KGB "maid" asked him, "How are you enjoying your stay in Soviet Union?"

Before Ludlow could answer, she said, "Please speak directly into flowerpot."

After that, Ludlow and I devised a brilliant code to use each time we knew somebody out there was listening.

Now that we are both safely out of the country and plan never to go back, here is one of our typical conversations while in the Soviet Union, followed by the translation:

LUDLOW: " 'Rosebud' in the third race at Pimlico." (I'm so tired of Russian food, I could eat a horse.)

ME: "This little piggy went to market." (Before I left home, I went by the Piggly Wiggly supermarket and picked up a couple of cans of pork and beans for the trip. Want some?)

LUDLOW: "Is a bear Catholic?" (In the name of God, yes.)

LUDLOW (again):   "Are you going to watch *Sanford and Son*?" (Are you as sick as I am of looking at all that junk in Russian museums?)

ME: "Roger. The big polar bear walks late." (Dang right. I'm going over to a bar tonight at a hotel where they are supposed to have ice.)

LUDLOW: "Is the new Sears Roebuck catalog in yet?" (You got any toilet paper left in your room?)

ME: "Pass the Charmin." (A little, but I'm in big trouble when that's gone.)

LUDLOW: "Does Bonzo have the key?" (Do you think President Reagan is correct in thinking these people are a major threat to the security of our nation?)

ME: "A flush beats a straight." (Are you kidding me? A country that still can't master the flush toilet couldn't hit its own foot with a guided missile.)

LUDLOW: "Shoot low, boys, they're ridin' Shetland ponies." (Have you noticed how squatty-looking all the Russian women are?)

ME: "The elephants are marching." (They all have big fat ankles, too.)

LUDLOW: "When the bird of paradise flies away, Santa's belly will roll like jelly." (When we finally blow this place, I'm going to be one happy fat man.)

ME: "Hey, Mabel, Black Label." (I'll drink to that).

LUDLOW: "Now's the time for all good men to come to the aid of their country." (Isn't it a little silly for two grown men to be sitting here talking like this?)

ME: "The quick brown fox jumped over the lazy brown dog."
(You can't be too careful when the security of your country is involved.)
LUDLOW: "Loose lips can sink ships, Jarhead." (That's the
first thing they told us at boot camp in Parris Island.)

Sex in Moscow

As I read the reports of the sex-for-secrets scandal involving marine guards at our embassy in Moscow and Russian
beauties, I kept wondering why I hadn't seen any women in
Russia to write home about when I was there.

I met a female conductor on a train. She could have pulled it.

I met a tour guide who had fat ankles and hairy calves. She
could curdle borscht.

The only woman I saw who had even the remotest chance
of getting secrets out of me was a performer at a Moscow
nightspot.

She came onstage in a Russian bikini (tank top and knee-
length exercise shorts) and entertained the crowd by twirling
eleven hula hoops around her waist for what seemed like an
hour and a half.

If hula hoops are still going over that big in the Soviet
Union, I thought to myself, wait until the Russians are introduced to Slinkies and Mr. Microphones.

Let me put it this way: If the women I saw were any indica-
tion of the beauty of the entire female population of the Soviet
Union, Tammy Faye Bakker could walk down a street in Moscow and dogs wouldn't growl at her.

I recently received a letter begging my pardon about all this, however.

I'm not at liberty to disclose the name of the letter's author for reasons that soon will be obvious, but I can tell you he is from Deep South Georgia and was in Moscow to help plan an agricultural exposition not so long ago.

The man writes of walking into his Moscow hotel for the first time and spotting a gaggle of lovely, well-dressed young ladies, who, he later learned by direct contact, were prostitutes.

I will allow him to describe what later occurred.

"I was drinking vodka in my room with this gorgeous Tanya who spoke fluent English and assured me she was a direct descendant of Princess Alexandra.

"We began discussing price, and she said I could not pay her in rubles because it was her duty to take only foreign currency in order to help the Russian economy. With foreign currency, she explained, the Soviets could import more foreign goods.

"I had purposely left only one traveler's check in my wallet," the letter continues.

"I pulled it out and told her, 'I'm just a poor old country boy from South Georgia, and all I've got is this one traveler's check.

"She started rebuttoning things and then she noticed a book of withdrawal slips from the First National Bank of Rabbit, Georgia, that was sitting on my night table.

"She said, 'You have more than one traveler's check. Look at all these.'

"I took a long gulp out of my vodka, smiled sweetly at her, and said, 'Princess, I think me and you are about to do wonders for the Russian economy.' "

In the Huddle with George Bush

George Bush and certain members of his staff were discussing America's schedule of military opponents for the upcoming Bush administration.

Scheduling opponents is just as important for countries as it is in football.

Hitler, for instance, made the mistake of scheduling too many difficult opponents. As long as his Germans were up against Poland and Czechoslovakia, no sweat.

But then Hitler decided to upgrade and schedule the Soviet Union and the United States. He lost both of those, so goodbye to the trip to the Löwenbräu–John Deere World Domination Bowl.

Anyway, back to Bush. "Anybody got any idea who we should open with?" the president asked.

"I'd say let's kick it off with Libya," offered Jack Kemp, the former professional quarterback. "Libya's been the Gipper's favorite opponent, and we can just about count on a win there. We shoot down a couple more of their jets and maybe drop a few bombs close to Qaddafi's house."

"Why don't we also blow up the controversial chemical plant Qaddafi is using to produce poisonous gases?" asked Elizabeth Dole.

"Stay out of this, Elizabeth," said Bush. "This is man talk.

"It's agreed, then," said Bush. "We open with Libya. Who's next?"

"Are there any more American medical students in Grenada we need to rescue from the Cubans?" asked James Baker.

"If not," said Kemp, "we can plant a few. Grenada would be a pushover, too, and we'd be two–oh and on our way."

"How 'bout a third opponent?" asked Bush.

"We need at least a fairly tough opponent in order to gain in the polls," suggested John Sununu.

"Iran?" asked Bush.

"Perfect," said Sununu. "We'll bomb a few offshore oil rigs and then blow a few armed Iranian patrol boats out of the water."

"Then," said Kemp, "we'll schedule Angola. Then we'll send in some more military advisers to help the Contras kick butt in Nicaragua. And I think we could get away with sending troops into Haiti to restore order."

"What if Haiti doesn't need its order restored?" asked Secretary Dole.

"For the last time, Elizabeth," interrupted Bush, "stay out of things you don't know anything about.

"We need four more opponents," Bush went on. "Any ideas, Danny?"

"What were we talking about again?" asked the vice-president.

"Elizabeth," said Bush, "would you and Danny please go get some sandwiches and coffee? We've got a lot of work to do here."

Those remaining in the conference put their heads together and came up with four more opponents for the United States military schedule.

Syria was picked for some offshore naval bombardment, and then it was agreed to send troops to El Salvador to stop the further spread of Communist influence in Central America.

It was also agreed to invade Iceland, just for the heck of it, and then end the season with a strong opponent where a win would add credibility to a perfect record.

Kemp suggested fighting Norway over fishing rights, Sununu came up with Mexico to stop dope and illegal immigrants, and

Baker got a wild idea and threw in Portugal, but nobody could think of anything to be mad at the Portuguese about.

So Bush finally settled the argument and decided to invade Canada in 1992 during the Democratic Convention because all that land should have been ours in the first place.

"The Gipper," beamed Kemp, "would be proud."

How 'Bout Them Japanese!

I thought I'd heard everything:

- Hosea Williams dropping a suit against the Ku Klux Klan
- Rock Hudson being gay
- Michael Dukakis admitting he's a liberal
- The Kremlin loosening up
- A pitcher of orange juice costing me $37.50 from room service in a New York hotel
- The Atlanta Falcons winning a game

But that's nothing compared to the news Coca-Cola wants Georgia and Georgia Tech to go play each other in football in Tokyo.

It was in the papers. I read it with my own eyes. It's probably not going to happen, because both schools say it's not feasible, but that the idea was even hatched is frightening.

What's going on here?

Oft I have warned about the Japanese influence on our

country. The Japanese even tried to buy Atlanta's Hartsfield Airport, and Mayor Andy Young even listened to the offer.

The Japanese have bought every American golf course that isn't nailed down, several tall buildings, and they'll probably do a deal and wind up owning Oregon and Lake Erie before it's over.

Georgia and Georgia Tech in Tokyo, indeed.

You think we were surprised at Pearl Harbor?

Can you imagine the Japanese reaction to ten or twenty thousand bulldogs barking at one another in a hotel lobby in Tokyo?

"Tora! Tora! Tora!" is one thing, but "How 'bout them Dawgs" is quite another.

And what on earth would fans do about the traditional tailgating parties before the game?

Is fried chicken that easy to find in Tokyo? And if it's not, if we cook our own and took it with us, would it spoil on the plane ride?

I talked to a few Georgia and Tech fans soon after the news of Coke's idea to switch the game. They were surprisingly warm to the idea.

Said Leroy Parsons, Georgia fan: "At least it would be a lot easier to get to Tokyo than it was to get to Starkville when we played Mississippi State."

Said Miles Purvis, Tech fan: "I'd rather go to Tokyo than back to Athens. Last time I was in Athens, a Georgia fan barked at me and bit my leg. It took me four hours to get home in all that traffic."

Offered Dorothy Sims, Georgia fan: "I'd rather go to Tokyo than back to Grant Field" (now Bobby Dodd Stadium).

"At least the rest rooms would probably be cleaner."

Countered Ruby Lesterfield, of a Tech persuasion: "I think it would be exciting. The only other time I've been overseas is when we took the kids to Canada."

Well, not me. We've tampered with enough traditions in

this country as it is, and I'm damned proud of our two major state schools who would not budge, and the Tech–Georgia game isn't going anywhere.

Move the game to Tokyo and the next thing you know, the Masters will move to Lisbon and Andy Young will uproot the dogwoods and replant them in Botswana.

Have You Heard of Boise, Idaho?

The wire services carried an article recently concerning a group of Western journalists and military personnel being given a closeup look at a strategic missile site inside the Soviet Union.

This, of course, had to do with the mutual inspection clause that was a part of the U.S./Soviet arms-reduction agreement.

One Soviet officer was quoted as saying, "I never would have believed there would have come a time when we would allow such an inspection of a missile site."

Hooray for Gorbachev. Hooray for Reagan. Hooray for glasnost. Hooray for anything that makes the world a little safer from getting blown to bits.

As I read further into the article, feeling pretty good about the chances of getting to live out my life, I came across a sentence I'd just as soon not have read.

"Even with arms reduction," the article said, "the Soviets still have enough missiles to destroy such major American cities as New York and Washington in a matter of minutes."

That was like taking a sip of a marvelous glass of wine and saying, "What a marvelous glass of wine," and having your dinner companion add, "Yeah, but now you're just one step closer to ruining your liver."

As I pondered all this a bit longer, I also began to ask myself, "Where would be the best place in the United States in which to live and feel fairly safe about not getting a direct Soviet missile hit?"

Certainly not in such major cities as New York and Washington. You read anything about Soviet military power and it always gets around to mentioning, ". . . to completely destroy such major American cities as New York and Washington in a matter of minutes."

It never reads, ". . . to completely destroy such major American cities as Dallas and Milwaukee in a matter of minutes."

I guess Dallas and Milwaukee would be okay, but there're some other places I would feel safe as well. I'll list a few and give the reasons why.

1. *Miami*—The Soviets don't dare shoot at Miami. They could be off target just a hair and hit Castro ninety miles away.
2. *Boise, Idaho*—I figure the Soviets have never even heard of Boise. A lot of Americans haven't, either, for that matter.
3. *San Diego*—Great weather, great zoo, and you could always grab your stuff and sit out the war drinking tequila in Mexico if L.A. were hit.
4. *Nashville, Tennessee*—Even the Evil Empire wouldn't shoot at Dolly Parton and Barbara Mandrell.
5. *Tulsa, Oklahoma*—That's where Oral Roberts lives. You could write him a check and he'd put in a good word for you when he talks to God.
6. *Cleveland*—Why would anybody want to waste a perfectly good missile on Cleveland?

As for me, I think I'll stay in Atlanta. The weather's good, the girls are pretty, they talk my language, and Atlanta has already hosted the Democratic Convention.

Isn't that enough punishment for one city?

They're Buying American—Literally

Several days ago, I began reading a book titled *December 7, 1941* by World War II historian Gordon Prange.

The book deals, in incredible detail, with the events of the day the Japanese pulled off their attack on the U.S. Fleet at Pearl Harbor.

I was up to the part where the Japanese air commander radioed "Tora! Tora! Tora!"—indicating to his superiors the attack was, in fact, going to be a complete surprise.

I put down my book at that point, however, because my morning paper had arrived.

On the front page, the headline screamed out at me: JAPANESE BUY IBM TOWER.

The next day there was another front-page story: JAPANESE EYE OTHER OFFICE TOWERS HERE.

As a native of Atlanta, Georgia, imagine how I felt. On the one hand, I had been deeply engrossed in reading how the sneaky Japanese blew us to hell and back at Pearl Harbor, while on the other I was learning the Japanese are trying to buy my hometown.

The situation reminded me of a lady friend of mine whose hobby was reading *Gone With the Wind*.

She had read the book over two hundred times and was a fierce defender of the South.

For some unexplained reason, however, she had married a man from Rhode Island, and their Atlanta neighbors were from Ohio.

One afternoon, her Rhode Island husband and his Ohio pal were working in her basement.

She was upstairs reading *GWTW* again and was at the point where the Yankee soldier is drooling at Scarlett. (It was his last drool, if you recall.)

Suddenly, her husband called to her from the basement.

"Honey," he said, "we're thirsty. Could you bring us some ice water?"

"Why don't you Yankee (bleeps) get your own damned water?" she fired back.

But more on the Japanese. It wasn't that long ago they tried to buy Atlanta's Hartsfield International Airport, and Mayor Andy Young actually considered the sale before he came to his senses.

The IBM Tower, a marvelous piece of architecture, has become the new star of Atlanta's skyline. Now, it belongs to the Japanese.

And they are said to be eyeing other Atlanta halls of commerce.

What will they want next? The Varsity? Will we be ordering fried fish heads instead of chili dogs sometime in the future?

Is anything safe from Japanese cash? If they can't buy Hartsfield Airport, are they now turning to Dobbins Air Force Base?

And if they are, what does that say to us?

Two guys were discussing foreign interests in the United States. One said to the other, "I'm afraid the Arabs are trying to buy America."

"Don't worry," his friend replied, "the Japanese won't sell it to them."

The Rising Sum Will Cost Us

So now we have a treaty with the Russians. Great. But what are we going to do about the Japanese?

Our trade imbalance with them was enough of a problem, but now the Japanese have come up with a new plan that's even sneakier than what they did on the Day of Infamy.

They're trying to buy our country. All of it.

They started off with golf resorts. The Japanese are striking at the very backbone of this great nation by buying up all the golf resorts.

There are not enough golf courses to go around for all the golfers in Japan. Joining a golf club in Japan requires a down payment of all your yen and then some, and you call the pro shop for tee times years in advance.

Ever play behind Japanese golfers? I have. They're slower than Gladys and Bernice who hit it three feet and won't pick up their ball if it takes them thirty shots to get it in the hole.

I heard a story about Japanese golfers. It was a Saturday at an American course and suddenly play came to a complete stop.

The ranger went out to find the problem and came upon a Japanese foursome. The problem was the Japanese had lost all but one ball.

Each player would hit the last ball, get in the cart, go out and mark it, and then return the ball for the next hitter.

They were hanged on a makeshift gallows near the practice tee.

They're taking over our golf courses, and now they're after our airports.

A group of Japanese have offered to buy Atlanta's Hartsfield Airport, which runs neck and neck with Chicago's O'Hare as the world's busiest.

And Andy Young, the mayor of Atlanta, said, "I think I ought to at least listen to their offer."

Andy, have you lost your mind? The Japanese get their hands on Atlanta's airport and they're in easy striking distance of Fort McPherson Army Base, Dobbins Air Force Base, and the Varsity.

Atlanta might make it without the two military bases, but nobody wants to go into the Varsity and order two chili dogs and have them topped with rice instead of onions. Plus, I can't imagine a Japanese person ever learning to say those magic, hallowed Varsity words, "Wadda ya have? Wadda ya have?"

Let's say we are stupid enough to sell the Japanese Atlanta's airport. What will they come after next?

They buy Nashville and take over country music. Instead of Willie Nelson, you'll be listening to Tex Wang singing, "I may be a Nip, but I shoot from the hip, come a ty ri ri, rippy rippy aaa . . ."

Country music goes down, then Kroger stores and K marts are next.

If John Wayne were still alive, he'd know what to do to the Japanese investors—take a seven iron and run them and their checkbooks back home before it's too late and Vanna White has to learn eight zillion character signs in the Japanese alphabet to keep her job.

13

WEIGHTY MATTERS

Putting Their Best Chins Forward

There was a story in the papers about a group that calls itself the National Association to Aid Fat Americans (NAAFA), holding a convention in Newark, New Jersey. (Why any group would hold a convention in Newark is beyond me when such glamorous convention sites as Dogpatch, U.S.A., and Booger Hollow in Eureka Springs, Arkansas, are available. I remain convinced that if you live in the Northeast and don't go to Sunday School, when you die you go to Newark.)

The story told of members of NAAFA wanting to convince other Americans that, despite the fact they are fat, they are quite happy.

They also want to tell their fellow Americans it's okay if someone refers to them as "fat."

"I don't like being called cuddly or chubby," said Mary Jane Grace-Brown, a member of NAAFA who weighs in at four hundred pounds.

"I like fat. It's a descriptive word, just like thin, tall, or small."

I know others who carry around a great deal of weight who feel the same way. My stepbrother, Ludlow Porch, a radio talk-show host, humorist, and author—and a bit full-figured himself—has written several books on the subject.

His first, *It's Not So Neat to See Your Feet*, was followed by *Thin May Be In, But Fat's Where It's At*, and *The History of the Toledo Scale Co.*

What really caught my eye in the article about the fatso—remember it's okay to say that—convention was the statement by Mrs. Grace-Brown's husband, James, who weighs 125 pounds, three times less than she does.

Mr. Brown, who married his wife at last year's convention, stated he loved her just the way she was and wouldn't have her any other way.

How intriguing, I thought to myself, when you consider how much time and money today's woman spends keeping her figure somewhere between anorexic and hollow-eyed and bird-legged.

They go through all this, I am certain, to be attractive to the male. But if Mr. Brown is satisfied with his wife at four hundred pounds, there must be advantages to taking up with a fat girl.

I have considered the following:

1. Fat girls probably appreciate their mates more than thin girls do because fat girls have spent a lot of time being snubbed. Cordie Mae Poovey, a girl in my school, was so fat she lived in two ZIP codes and nobody would date her.
2. Fat girls won't serve you Lean Cuisine, Jerusalem artichokes, or bean sprouts for supper. Just make certain you get to the mashed potatoes before they do.
3. Snuggle up to a fat girl when you go to sleep at night and think what you could save in insulation costs for your house.

I am not certain, incidentally, whether or not Cordie Mae is a member of NAAFA, but she finally did find a husband, one of the Phillpot boys who didn't weigh what her big toe did.

When asked how it was living with a fat girl, the Phillpot boy answered, "Every time I think I have done loved all of Cordie Mae, I find new, uncharted territory."

That's another way of saying, God bless fat girls. There's just more of them to love.

Where Do All Those Lost Pounds Go?

In the wake of the astounding news that television star Oprah Winfrey has lost sixty-seven pounds and actually can squeeze into a pair of jeans that didn't come from a tent and awning company, there's something I've often wondered about:

When a person loses weight, where does the weight go? It has to go somewhere, doesn't it?

I have a few theories in this area, and I will share them with you in hopes of perhaps gaining some enlightenment.

One thought I've had is that when a person loses weight, it evaporates up into the atmosphere somewhere.

We worry about acid rain and losing the ozone layer, but what about all that fat that may be up there if my theory is correct?

Is there in fact a danger that Americans are losing so much weight these days the accumulated fat might all cling together up in the heavens and eventually block out the sun?

Oprah lost enough weight by herself to block out several Ohio cities, not to mention all of Dade County, Florida.

I'm not saying Oprah was grossly obese, but it's no secret that high school football coaches often called to see if she would allow their squads to get into shape by running laps around her.

Okay, so all that lost weight doesn't go into the atmosphere. But is it still around somewhere lurking in hidden places waiting to jump on somebody else?

I gained a lot of weight during my college days. I went from a 140-pound high school senior to a 200-pound college junior.

At first, doctors thought I had swallowed a Volkswagen Beetle.

However, that turned out not to be true. I also hadn't changed my diet that significantly, so all that weight must have come off another person. It is interesting to note that I sat next to a large girl in history class my sophomore year of college.

She came back as a junior quite petite, and there I was, a blowfish.

I eventually took off all that extra weight, and my body regained the slim, athleticlike form it has today.

During the time I was losing my weight, a neighbor gained thirty pounds. Was that merely a coincidence?

All that dieting and exercising people do today could be a little stupid if this particular theory of mine is correct.

You could be leaving your health club after a workout and run into some homeless fat. Just like that, you wouldn't be able to get your leotards any higher than your ankles.

My final theory is that losing weight is sort of like giving birth.

Oprah Winfrey lost sixty-seven pounds. Does that mean that somewhere there's a little sixty-seven pound Oprah-clone running around trying to get interviews with gay porn stars?

And what if that sixty-seven pound Oprah eventually puts on a lot of weight and then sheds it? If this process were to continue, we could be up to our ears in Oprah Winfreys, and there aren't enough cable stations to handle that many.

This is all merely conjecture, of course, but it's something to think about during the holiday season.

Will that cheese ball or fruitcake you're gnawing on one day help block out the sun or jump on some unsuspecting innocent skinny person? Or will it take on a life of its own?

Perhaps someday science will provide an answer. Meanwhile, on the next *Grizzard:* Famous People with Flat Noses.

Cordie Mae's
Gain-Weight Diet

Everybody and his fat sister-in-law is trying to lose weight.

I must see fifteen different diet programs advertised during just one night of television.

That's fine, but aren't there some people out there who want to *gain* weight? I see skinny people everyday.

These people look pale, sickly, underfed, and they couldn't be happy looking like that.

But nobody helps them. Nobody offers a gain-weight diet. At least I haven't seen one, so I've decided to help.

I phoned an old schoolmate of mine, the former Cordie Mae Poovey, who still weighs more than the mobile home in which she lives with her devoted husband, Hog Philpott.

(Hog's no lightweight himself. Down at Mudd's Gulf, where he works, they refer to Hog as "Al." Al as in Alps.)

As for Cordie Mae, the stork didn't bring her. UPS did. It took the entire plane.

Cordie Mae can look at a bowl of mashed potatoes and

sprout a new forty-five-pound arm. She tried to visit Rhode Island once, but they wouldn't let her in. There wasn't enough room.

(I would steal Rodney Dangerfield's line here, but I'm not that kind of person. So I'll give him credit for saying he went out with a girl who was so fat, when she wore watches on each of her wrists they were in different time zones.)

I told Cordie Mae of the plight of skinny people, and she agreed to share her countywide, famous "When-Your-Arms-Get - Tired - of - Shoveling - in - the - Food - Then - Eat - With - Your-Feet-Bloatation Diet."

"Just give us a typical one-week program," I said.

"I'd be happy to," said Cordie Mae, reaching into her icebox for a quart of lard on which to snack while she dictated her gain-weight diet. Clip and save the following:

Monday   Breakfast, a dozen eggs, six cinnamon rolls, a chocolate cake, then go to Shoney's for the breakfast buffet. Lunch, a jar of mayonnaise, three Wendy's double cheeseburgers, four grape snow cones, and a gross of Butterfingers. Dinner, a barbecued goat, hold the mayo. You've had enough of that for lunch.

Tuesday   Breakfast, a dozen chocolate Dove bars, a liter of Pepsi, and whatever was left of the barbecued goat. Lunch, call Domino's for pizza. Order their entire inventory. Dinner, a Waffle House.

Wednesday   Breakfast, a tub of grits (with butter), four vanilla milkshakes and one pork chop for every year you've been able to vote. Lunch, all the pork chops you want, no limit. Dinner, what the heck. Eat another barbecued goat.

Thursday   Breakfast, a dozen Twinkies, and then go to Baskin-Robbins for some real food. Lunch, some munchies from Kroger. The entire aisle. Dinner, a gallon of mashed potatoes and a banana-split salad.

Friday   Breakfast, two boxes of donuts, and a jar of peanut butter mixed with whipped cream. Lunch, fill up the back of your truck at the McDonald's drive-through window. Dinner, one large buffalo cooked any way you want.

Saturday   Just lie around the trailer all day and relax with a vat of banana pudding.

Sunday   A day of rest. Send your husband or wife out for tacos and stop by the Chinese place for egg rolls, and then go to the deli for potato salad and cheesecake. And if a chicken walks through your house, knock it in the head and fry it in case the Colonel is closed when you need a midnight snack.

Cordie Mae says good luck—and good gaining.

14

BAD
HABITS

Hints for Sobriety

A lot of people are turning away from alcohol these days, including my friend Rigsby, the former lush, who phoned to tell me of his plans to give up drinking.

"How long have you been drinking?" I asked him.

"Professionally, twenty-five years," he said.

"What is the difference between a professional and an amateur drinker?"

"A professional," Rigsby began, "drinks every night except New Year's Eve, which is amateur night. A professional never drinks anything with an umbrella or a cherry in it, and a professional awakens at least ten times a year in a Holiday Inn in a different time zone and doesn't remember getting there."

For others who may be considering stopping drinking, I asked Rigsby for some telltale signs one should look for in determining whether or not one has stepped over the quaffing line.

"It's the morning after that says it all," Rigsby said.

"Start with your tongue. If you have to shave it, then you had way too much to drink the night before.

"Then there's your money. Look at any bills you might have left over, and if they have been wadded into tiny little balls and you find them in strange places like your shoe or your ear, son, you got down to some serious drinking the night before."

"What else?" I asked.

"Check your clothing. Did you remember to take it off before you passed out? Check to make certain the clothing you have on is the same clothing you had on when you left for the evening.

"If you are wearing a fez, it was a big night. If you are wearing a Royal Canadian Mountie's hat, then you had an even bigger night.

"And if the Mountie's horse is down in the living room, grazing on house plants, call AA immediately and see if they deliver, because you won't be able to get anywhere in your condition.

"There's a few other things to look for, too," Rigsby continued.

- "Check any credit-card receipts you can find, if they are for charges at a Frederick's of Hollywood, at an arms dealer, or with a foreign airline, you've got troubles.
- "Look at your checkbook. If checks 1562 through 1568 are missing and you don't remember writing them, call the bank and stop payment as soon as you are able to operate a telephone.
- "And this one is very important: Check your body for any unexplained tattoos.

"If you find one you didn't have before and it's a heart with an arrow through it and includes the names Doris, Trixie, Mona, or Grover, make up your mind to stop drinking forever, but call your attorney first."

I thanked Rigsby for his hints and I hope they have been a public service.

To sobriety, then. It just might catch on.

Would You Walk a Mile for One?

Right in the middle of the current focus on making everybody quit smoking and making those who don't quit feel terribly guilty, one of the giants of cigarettedom is having a birthday.

Perhaps you have seen the billboards proclaiming the seventy-fifth anniversary for Camels, once known in various circles of mine as "the man's cigarette."

For those who never smoked, allow me to explain:

Some years ago, somebody came up with the idea to put filters on cigarettes. The idea was, the filter would remove some of the tar and nicotine and whatever else it is that will kill you if you smoke.

Filters also made the tobacco taste a little milder, and most everybody eventually began smoking filtered cigarettes. A few hardy souls held on, however, and continued to smoke unfiltered, to-hell-with-it cigarettes like Camels.

I remember pulling out a pack of filtered Marlboros over a few beers during my college days.

The man sitting next to me thrust a pack of Camels in my face and said, "Here, smoke a man's cigarette."

It clearly would have been a sign of weakness had I not taken the fellow's offering.

I put a light to the end of the Camel and inhaled deeply. I sucked in several loose leaves of tobacco, burned my tongue, and couldn't speak for fifteen minutes.

Still, I always admired Camel smokers. I like the short little

Camel pack and the way a Camel smoker would hit one end of the cigarette on the table or on his lighter in order to compact the tobacco leaves, making the Camel even stronger.

I also liked the Camel package itself. It was mostly brown and there was a picture of a camel, of course, and there used to be a game to see who could find the most *E*s on a Camel package.

I don't know many people who smoke at all anymore, much less people who smoke Camels. In fact, I can only think of two Camel smokers who are still alive. One is a college professor. Another is a newspaperman. They look well enough.

Seventy-five years people have been smoking Camels, huh?

The following story was told to me as truth:

There was a ninety-year-old man living in the North Carolina mountains who had allegedly smoked two packs of Camels a day since he was fifteen years old.

R. J. Reynolds, which makes Camels, heard of the man and sent a representative to see him.

The Reynolds man asked if the old boy would come to Winston-Salem, North Carolina (Reynolds's headquarters), to make a commercial.

They would show antismokers that you could smoke and still live a long life. The old man agreed to make the commercial.

"Can you be in Winston-Salem at nine Friday morning?" he was asked.

"Nope," said the old man.

"Why not?" asked the Reynolds man.

" 'Cause I don't quit coughing until twelve."

Happy anniversary, Camels.

How I Quit Smoking

You can't smoke anymore on New York commuter trains, and it probably won't be very long until you can't smoke anywhere.

You probably can't smoke where you work now, and restaurants and planes are also becoming smoke-free.

What happened is the antismokers, obnoxious though they can be, have won, and smokers have become outcasts and subjects of much derision.

If you smoke, there is only one plausible thing left for you to do.

You must quit.

I know. This comes from a man who smoked his head off for years and loved every cigarette he ever had.

Smoking was one of the great pleasures of my life. A cigarette was like a little reward I gave myself twenty-five to forty times a day.

But I quit. For several reasons:

- I've already had two heart-valve replacement surgeries and may one day face another. I need to smoke like I need getting poked in the eye with a sharp stick.
- Very few of my friends smoke anymore. I began to feel uncomfortable smoking in front of them.
- I fly 150 times a year. Airlines are turning off the smoking lights.
- Flying makes me nervous enough as it is without also craving a cigarette.
- None of my friends believed I really had the courage to stop smoking. I quit to prove them wrong.

Here's how I did it, after smoking for twenty-three years:

- I made a pact with three friends that we would stop smoking together.
- I figured at least one of them wouldn't make it and I could start again, too. But they all stayed smokeless and I hung in there with them.
- When the craving was at its worst, I kept telling myself, "Nobody ever died from stopping smoking."
- I also relied on others who quit long ago who said to me, "I know it's hard for you to believe now, but there will come a time you won't even think of a cigarette anymore."

  It took me three weeks to reach the point where I actually had a thought other than having a cigarette.
- I substituted eating ice cream for smoking. I put on fifteen quick pounds and made the Häagen-Dazs people rich, but it still helped me quit smoking.

I became an obnoxious nonsmoker myself. I berated a man (a small man) for lighting up in a nonsmoking area of an Amtrak train and I bragged to friends who continued to smoke after I quit: "Well, all I can say is, I'm glad I'm no longer a slave to tobacco."

If I ever start again, I would have to face much finger-pointing and ridicule. That gives me strength to carry on.

I gave myself an out. I'm going to start smoking again on my ninetieth birthday.

Quit, dammit.

Going Up in Smoke

My friend Rigsby, the entrepreneur, currently is hatching another of his get-rich-quick schemes.

He sounded excited when he told me about his idea over lunch.

"You heard smoking is now banned on all commercial flights in California, didn't you?" he asked.

I said I had. There was a near riot aboard a TWA jet when smokers rebelled against the new antismoking law.

"And things are just going to get worse," Rigsby went on. "After April, smokers will not be allowed to light up on any flight anywhere in the country of two hours or less. There are going to be a lot of uncomfortable smokers flying around up there."

I agreed, but I wanted to know where all this fits in with Rigsby's new idea.

"An all-smokers' airline." He beamed.

"I don't understand," I said.

"It's simple," Rigsby explained. "I'm going to lease some airplanes and start a new airline for smokers only.

"You can smoke all you want on my airline. In fact, I will encourage smoking. Flight attendants will carry cigarettes up and down the aisle like the girls in Vegas. I'll charge five bucks a pack. A smoker who runs out of cigarettes on an airplane is a desperate individual who will pay anything for another pack."

I admitted the idea had some promise.

"What are you going to call your airline?" I asked Rigsby.

"I've got my marketing staff on that now," he said. "We're thinking of something that will really catch the smoking public's attention. 'Black Lung Airlines' was one thought."

"I don't think so," I said.

"Then how about 'Air Emphysema'?"

"Keep trying."

"Okay," said Rigsby, "but let me tell you what else I'm going to offer on my all-smokers' airline.

"First we're going to make certain no nonsmokers come aboard and make life miserable for our customers. We will check each passenger's teeth and fingers. If they aren't yellow from smoking, they don't get a boarding pass.

"We're not going to fly high enough to need cabin pressurization, so our passengers won't have to worry about ever having to use those oxygen masks and not being able to smoke.

"Our flight crew will all be smokers, as well as our flight attendants, mechanics, reservationists, and boarding agents."

"But," I asked, "won't all that smoking make it uncomfortable on the plane?"

"Of course not," said Rigsby. "Smokers love smoke, and we're going to issue a miner's hat with the little light on the front so passengers can find the lavatories regardless of how thick the smoke is in the cabin."

"When will your ad campaign begin?" I asked my friend.

"Shortly," he said.

"What's your hook?"

"It's a great one—'An all-smokers' airline, here to serve you just in the nick of teen.' "

Who am I to scoff? They laughed at Wilbur and Orville, too.

Six Steps to Stop Smoking, Butt Don't Stumble

Since I wrote of my successful effort in quitting smoking, I have had many letters and calls.
They fit into two categories:

- One group said, "You lying sleazebag. You didn't quit smoking."
- The other group wanted to know, "How on earth did a weak individual such as yourself find the self-control to quit smoking?"

I will address the first group by saying, "Yes, I did quit smoking. I still want a cigarette, I dream about cigarettes, and if anybody comes out with a cigarette that won't kill me, I'll start smoking them again."

I want to answer the second group by replying, "Even the weakest individuals, such as me, can quit smoking, too, if they follow my step-by-step stop-smoking plan, which is absolutely free and doesn't involve chewing any gum or taking any shots or medicine or getting hypnotized."

Here is how to quit smoking, my way:

- *Step 1:* Get aboard some type of public conveyance that doesn't allow smoking and light up a cigarette. When nonsmokers begin to harass you, ignore them and keep on smoking.

Nonsmokers are violent, revenge-bent people. At some point, one of these people will come over to you, take your cigarette out of your mouth, crush it on the floor, and hit you somewhere in the region of your head.

Also realize it won't be that much longer until non-smokers will begin shooting smokers in the streets. Now, you're on the way to being smoke-free.

- *Step 2:* Soon the stitches are out and your bruises are healed, but you're getting the urge to smoke again.

  Buy a pack of cigarettes, take one out of the pack, and light it. Now, instead of putting the unlit end in your mouth, do it the other way. It will take those blisters on your tongue weeks to heal, and during that period, you won't want a cigarette.

- *Step 3:* The next time you get the urge to smoke, go buy a pack of Larks. I'm not even certain they make Larks anymore, so if you can't find a pack, try smoking a piece of shag carpet instead—it's about the same thing.

- *Step 4:* Invite Surgeon General Koop over for dinner. After eating, light up a cigarette and explain how much casual sex you've been having lately, and how you think condoms are a silly waste of time. The Surgeon General will begin screaming at you and breaking up your furniture. This man is serious about cigarettes and condoms.

- *Step 5:* Recall that John Wayne smoked; and cigarettes got him when 8 zillion Japanese couldn't.

- *Step 6:* The final step. Before going to bed one evening, open a beer and drink half of it.

Then light a cigarette and smoke it and throw the butt into the half-empty beer can. In fact, smoke a couple more cigarettes and put them out in the beer can.

Let it sit overnight.

The next morning before you do anything else, find the can and take a big swallow of the warm beer with the soggy cigarettes in it.

If you still want to smoke after that, then there's nothing I, or anybody else, can do for you, Pilgrim.

15

OF TIME
AND
BIRTH

Children Are Forever

Two very close friends of mine recently became fathers for the first time.

Another friend's wife is scheduled to deliver their first child soon.

All three of these men are forty or older.

"It's never too late," each has said to me at one time or the other during their wives' pregnancies.

I guess they're right. I'm forty-one, been down one time, two times, and three times in marriage, but as far as I know, I have held on to my ability to father a child.

We actually tried in my first marriage, but there was a problem she later overcame with medical help. Now, with her new husband, she is the mother she always wanted to be.

Second time was a whirlwind. Third time, she already had two, one out in the playroom screaming, the other outside riding his Big Wheel.

Ever hear the sound a Big Wheel—a plastic tricycle—makes as it is pedaled across a driveway?

Severe nervous breakdowns have been spawned from less.

"Men," a wise person once said to me, "often want children to satisfy their egos. They want to look down in that crib and say, 'Hey, that's my boy!'

"They look upon their children as proof of their manhood, and as their link with immortality, but some never quite understand the responsibility that comes with being a father to a child.

"It takes a real grown-up to be a good parent. And some men never really grow up."

I've thought about those words often, especially lately when previously childless friends suddenly turned fruitful and multiplied.

Why would I really want a child? To satisfy my ego? To leave a living monument?

To have something I could love without conditions and be loved in return in the same manner? (That sort of thing is difficult to find, you know.)

In order to be the father I never really had? To be able to pass along what I have learned, what I think to be the truth and the way?

But a number of things stand between me and fatherhood. Number one being the fact I'm not married.

But even if I did marry again, I'd probably still think twice about children.

I've proved I'm not a good marriage risk. I came from a broken home. I don't want my child to have to do the same.

There remain childlike tendencies in my own repertoire. I have not quite given up on the idea of finding the ultimate party, and sometimes I have trouble giving up the night.

And there is the fact most things have an escape clause. You can leave a bad marriage, a bad job, and a city where the sun never shines. But children are forever.

What I could do rather than have children of my own is become the friendly uncle to my three buddies' children.

I could joke with them and bring them small gifts and enjoy their company while I am around them and then split with no responsibility for them when the spirit moves me.

I'd miss the "goodnight-daddy's," but I also wouldn't have to put up with strange, loud music coming from the upstairs bedroom and explaining to my son if he didn't take off that earring, I would cut him out of the will.

This entire discussion, quite frankly, has made me nervous. Maybe I'll bring it up again next year.

Memories of My Father

I was on a call-in radio show in Birmingham, Alabama. When you write a book, they make you travel and do call-in radio shows. Publicity is my life.

We were in the second hour in Birmingham. A lady had complained about something I'd written about Oral Roberts, somebody else wanted to know if I planned to get married again, and then a man called and said he knew my late father.

"He taught me in high school in Atlanta," the man said. "He was an unforgettable character."

Indeed. A number of people have contacted me over the years and said they had come across Lewis, Sr.

One such person called and said, "Your daddy owes me three hundred dollars. I let him borrow it in Kingsport, Tennessee, in 1962."

After informing the individual of my father's demise, I asked him, "How long did you know my father before you lent him the three hundred dollars?"

"About an hour," was the reply.

"My good man," I said, "you are one of many with the same experience."

My father was a lot of things, but more than anything else, he was a soldier. He served in World War II and in Korea. The Purple Hearts and the Bronze Star he earned hang on my office wall.

In Korea, his outfit was overrun by the Chinese communists. He survived by hiding under dead comrades and later by hiding for sixteen days in a cave, as his enemy walked about him.

When he finally made it back to the American lines, his feet were severely frostbitten, he was suffering from malnutrition, and he would never again be the man who went off to war a second time in 1950.

He returned home to Fort Benning. I was four. He drank heavily. He screamed out in the night. Eventually, he left my mother and went AWOL and spent the rest of his life roaming, drinking, and living off his considerable charm.

I have no idea how many different jobs my daddy held between the time he left the army and his death in 1970, but somehow he always managed to be able to get a teaching position whenever he wanted one.

"Your daddy," the man on the radio told me, "would make us laugh with all his carryings-on, and he would tell us about what happened to him in the war.

"And the thing I remember most was how he used his experience to teach us never to give up no matter how bad things looked.

"He said there were times in Korea he felt it would just be easier on him to die than to live in the situation he was in.

"He told us how his feet were swollen and bleeding and how he was afraid to move in that cave because the enemy might find him. But he said he just made up his mind he wasn't going to die out there, and that's what pulled him through."

We'd been on the line a long time. I thanked the caller, but he had more.

"I was in Vietnam," he said. "I was wounded and was left behind in a hot landing zone.

"I didn't know if anybody was coming back for me or if the enemy would find me. But I hid myself and I held on and I got out of there.

"I wanted to give up, too, but I kept thinking about your father. If Captain Grizzard could make it, I told myself, so could I. I give him credit for my being alive today. He was a great man."

I thanked the caller one more time—for perhaps the best Christmas gift I've ever had.

Of Time and Birth

A friend of mine became a father for the first time last week. He's even older than I am.

Yesterday, we were sitting on the front porch of the fraternity house drinking beer. Today, he's got a son.

I remember what the old folks used to say: "Lord, where does the time go?"

I didn't understand them then. I do now.

So we talked about his kid.

"He's got more hair now than I do," said my friend, whose bald spot showed up four or five years ago.

"How big was he when he was born?" I asked.

"Eight pounds, eleven ounces. He's going to be a big 'un."

"Did you get to hold him right after he was born?"

"Yeah, I had to scrub up, and then I got to hold him. That's when I really realized I had a son. That's when the bonding really takes place between father and son."

We never talked about it, but I always assumed my friend had his heart set on a boy child.

He's an ex-jock who still is competitive as ever on a tennis court, the golf course, or in his den throwing darts.

He had a wild streak in him when he was younger, and a lot of lovely ladies stood by with broken hearts and watched him go.

He was the best dancer who ever shagged to "Stubborn Kind of Fellow" back in school. He drove a red 1950 Chevy convertible and voted for Barry Goldwater.

After school, he flew airplanes, went to a war, went into business, and built a home the size of a small town.

A man like that wants a son.

His wife wanted him in the room with her when she bore him his child.

"I guess you were pretty happy when you saw it was a boy," I said to him.

"It wasn't like that," he said. "My thoughts were more with my wife than with anything else. She was a trouper."

"You mean she was in a lot of pain?"

"Let me put it to you this way—if it were up to me and you to have babies, there wouldn't be very many around."

I was impressed with his concern for his wife taking precedence over anything else. Knowing him, knowing me, knowing how much a son would mean to him, and knowing the general insensitivity of most men, I sensed a friend entering another phase of his life.

One where a man comes to peace with himself, there's the

wind to move him an inch, and he knows, without doubt, that in wife and child he has the only treasures that really matter anyway.

I used to laugh at such. Now, I'm jealous of it.

Lord, where does the time go?

16

GETTING OLDER

Life Calls No Time-Outs

I won't forget Friday, March 6, 1987, the day I finally was convinced the aging process had taken its toll upon me.

I didn't want to accept that. I turned forty in October 1986 but I noted at the time I felt about the same as I did when I turned eighteen.

My likes and dislikes hadn't changed. I still liked country music, and I still didn't like English peas.

And I danced the night of my fortieth away, and my partner, younger than I was, complimented me on a number of my moves.

"I may be worn," sings the Outlaw, Waylon Jennings, "but I ain't worn out."

Then, Friday, March 6, 1987.

I had been invited to participate in a halftime show at the Southeastern Conference basketball tournament.

I was to shoot free throws against a man named Ted St. Martin, the world's greatest free-throw shooter. You can look it up.

The opportunity to show off my pure shooting eye in front of thousands of people was an exciting one. I bragged to my friends, "I was a legendary free-throw shooter in high school."

"Are you going to practice?" I was asked.

"Of course not," I replied, "I can still get up on Christmas morning and hit eight of ten without warming up."

I honestly believed that.

I walked onto the court in Atlanta's OMNI as a hushed crowd watched.

Mr. St. Martin handed me the ball.

I remembered my technique. Hold the ball lightly with the fingers. Take a deep breath. Fix the eyes on the front of the rim on the basket. Bend the knees and release, following through with the flick of the wrist.

I missed my first three shots. The ball didn't feel like I remembered a basketball feeling. The shots came off my hands like bricks rather than butterflies.

I made my fourth shot, despite the fact that the ball hit several tons of metal. My fifth shot was the dreaded "airball." It hit nothing but the floor.

The crowd, turning hostile, chanted "Airball! Airball!"

Disgrace.

I wound up hitting four of ten. Mr. St. Martin didn't miss.

As I left the court, I am certain I heard boos.

I've taken a lot of ribbing.

"Hello, 'Deadeye,' " my friends have said, laughing.

"All hat, no cattle," others have observed.

"But twenty years ago . . ." I tried to explain.

"Twenty years ago," I was interrupted, "we all could do a lot of things better than we can now."

There's another way of saying that: Never let your mind write a check your body can't cash.

Truth. How sharply it can sting.

Now Ear This

I discovered something about myself recently that was quite unsettling. I discovered I have hair growing out of my ears, a sure sign of aging.

Once I turned forty, I naturally expected certain manifestations of the aging process.

The slight hint of crow's-feet are developing on each side of my mouth, I found a gray hair on my chest the other day, and I dozed off recently while watching the Playboy Channel on cable.

But I didn't expect ear hair for at least a few more years.

It probably has something to do with the fact that I don't eat yogurt and still prefer white bread to whole wheat.

To be certain it wasn't being caused by something else, however, I called the Dr. Ruth Show, to ask if this condition was connected to any sort of hormonal change in my body that might affect, well, certain activities.

"Of course not, my dear," answered Dr. Ruth.

"Many of my patients have had very satisfying sex lives after the development of ear hair. It is important, however, to keep the hair trimmed, not only to remain physically appealing to the opposite sex, but also to avoid any hearing impairment."

Relieved to hear that good news, I shaved inside my ears, put on my tightest jeans, and hit a couple of singles' bars.

I completely struck out, but at least I was able to hear when a nineteen-year-old girl with orange hair, who was wearing high-top tennis shoes, looked at me and said, "Like, wow, did you know your ears are bleeding?"

From now on, I am going to use a pair of scissors to trim my ear hair and forget the razor.

Too bad Van Gogh didn't think of that before it was too late.

Heavy ear hair does run in my family. My grandfather had ear hair at a relatively early age.

He allowed his to grow unchecked, which probably had a lot to do with the fact that he often suffered sudden losses of hearing whenever my grandmother asked him to perform such chores as putting on a tie for church and spreading manure on her rosebushes.

After much thought concerning the hair in my own ears, I have concluded it is important that I accept the fact that I am aging.

I enjoyed the springtime of my life. I made a few mistakes, but I had me some high times and I made me some memories.

But now that I am entering the autumn of my years, I want to enter gracefully.

I can't run as fast or jump as high as I once could, but in the immortal words of my grandfather, "The best thing about getting older is you don't have to put up with nearly as much manure as you once did."

So, onward on my voyage to senior citizenry despite the fact that I may follow in my grandfather's footsteps and allow my ear hair to grow unchecked.

When you get really old, it doesn't matter if you have so much hair in your ears: They both resemble a picture I saw once in a history book of President Rutherford B. Hayes.

Roy Orbison's Legacy

So there was this girl. I was fourteen and in love with her. I sat behind her in one of my classes and she used to wear those pretty sundresses and I'd just stare at her back.

I had known her since the sixth grade. She was gangly and awkward back then. She seemed to list a bit to starboard when she walked, and I used to think her mother dressed her funny.

But she changed. It was an incredible metamorphosis, I remember thinking. Well, maybe I didn't know the term "metamorphosis" back then, but one day she seemed put together without much thought; and the next, every part of her went nicely with the others.

Somebody had gotten to her before I made my own move. He was bigger than I was. He was a better athlete.

He was already shaving every day, and I was still a twice-a-week man. He had a friend who had a driver's license, and he could take the girl on double dates to the drive-in.

I had no access to wheels that my mother didn't drive. There is no shame like having your mother drive you and your date to the theater and then pick you up afterward.

I had all but abandoned hope, but then I heard Roy Orbison sing that song "Pretty Woman."

It was about a guy who saw a lady and fell for her.

But he had no chance. "Pretty woman, walk on by. . . ."

I know how you feel, friend.

"But what's this I see? . . ." he sang on. "Is she walkin' back to me?"

I might have given up if Roy Orbison hadn't sung that song. Roy Orbison certainly was no day at the beach to look at—and I wasn't, either—but in song, the pretty woman chose him.

I hung in there.

There was a church function one Saturday night, and the girl was there without her boyfriend.

I'm still not certain how it all came to pass, but we wound up on a hay wagon together. (There used to be things called "hayrides" back in another century. It was pretty exciting stuff in those days.)

I'm not sure if I kissed her first or if she kissed me. But I won't forget that kiss, ever.

Ten years later, we said good-bye, but it had been a fine ten years, full of more good times than bad, and if we hadn't rushed things, it might have lasted.

When the radio station I listen to began playing Roy Orbison songs after he died the other day, I heard "Pretty Woman" again and again, and each time, some old feelings came around and I even went back over some old regrets.

To leave something like music that stirs an emotion or makes a memory certainly isn't immortality, but it's about as close as we can come.

Roy Orbison was fifty-two. That's not nearly as old as it used to be.

Cheers for a Real-Life Bar

Harrison's, the bar on Peachtree Street, has closed. The end came New Year's Eve. A few of my friends and I, all former Harrison's regulars, stopped by and had one last toast. Okay, three or four last toasts.

"If these walls could talk," somebody said.

"I'd be divorced," said another.

Harrison's was in business more than a decade, which is a long time for a bar in a trendy city like Atlanta.

Call it what you will. A meat market? Sure. There is no accounting for the number of one-night stands, three-week flings, and even marriages—and for certain, divorces—that were started in Harrison's.

When it opened in the early seventies, there was no such thing as Yuppies. The clientele was young, and upwardly mobile to be certain—lots of Xerox salesmen in three-piece suits—but there was no name for us at the time.

We simply needed a meeting place, and Harrison's was it. On Friday nights, they were stacked ten-deep at the bar, and the young things in sundresses who had migrated to the city could take a young man's breath away.

The Harrison's legends are many. There was the guy who fell asleep in the men's room. He awakened at five in the morning, and in his attempt to leave, he set off the burglar alarm.

"Hi, guys," he said to the SWAT team that soon followed.

A man brought a lion into the joint one night and it sat down on a barstool next to him. What does a lion drink in a singles' bar? Anything he wants to.

Celebrities and would-be celebrities who were in the city always stopped by Harrison's. I spotted Forrest Tucker one night.

"Look," I said to a much younger companion, "there's Forrest Tucker."

"Who's Forrest Tucker?" she asked.

My favorite Harrison's story concerned a married man who was in most every night. He ran the ladies hard, but he had few successes.

One night, he did manage to make initial contact, and as he sat at a darkened table with his prey, the door to Harrison's opened and in ran three children in their pajamas.

They found their daddy and said to him, "Mommy's outside. She wants you to kiss us good night because you're never home to do it."

The hole he dug for himself, somebody said on closing night, is still over by that table.

When I moved to Chicago for three years, I missed Harrison's terribly. I would call on lonely Friday nights. The crowd noise in the background was soothing.

I don't know exactly what made Harrison's go under. Yeah, I do.

Atlanta has exploded in population over the past several years, and as the Harrison's regulars got older, the incoming nightlife crowd got younger and had no loyalty to any one spot with all the new bars with their Margarita nights and laser shows.

So the end has come for Harrison's, where I admittedly misspent a large portion of my youth. A lady I once knew might say of the closing, "Ten years too late."

When I Danced on the Ceiling

Each time I visit Savannah, Georgia, I recall the spring of 1963 when I was there, a boy of sixteen, and the azaleas were in bloom.

I was a member of the Key Club at my high school. I don't recall exactly what being in the Key Club involved, but I was a member of it and felt accepted, and that makes growing up a lot easier.

They held a state Key Club Convention here in Savannah that year, and I went. Some of us bought some beer and drank it in our hotel rooms.

We also went to one of the convention meetings out of curiosity, and a boy from Atlanta who wore thick glasses and pants that were too short gave a speech on the importance of being good representatives of our schools, communities, and parents while we were out of town.

I felt a little guilty about the beer, but the feeling soon passed.

Who else went to the state convention that year was our Key Club sweetheart. Every Key Club chapter had a sweetheart. I'm not sure why that was, either, but it made sense twenty-four years ago.

Our sweetheart had red hair and I was in love with her and our principal knew what he was doing when he made her stay in a different hotel than the boys in our group.

I had tried to get somewhere with our sweetheart before, but I always stammered and looked down at my feet a lot when I tried to talk to her.

Normally, I never said a lot of "uh's" and "ah's" and "you know's" in conversation, but when I tried to talk to our red-headed sweetheart I always sounded like a baseball player being interviewed on television.

"I, uh, ah, you know, I, you know, I, uh, you know . . ." I would begin, and by that time she and her red hair would be looking for somebody without an apparent speech impediment.

But there was that one glorious time in Savannah at the state Key Club Convention.

There was a dance contest, and you don't have to talk when you dance.

Members drew straws to see who would get to dance with our sweetheart in the contest.

I won.

There were maybe fifty couples entered in the contest.

The band played "Stay," by Maurice Williams and the Zodiacs.

My partner and I were one of four finalists. And then there was only one other couple to challenge us.

My feet were winged and I was rhythm and grace, elegance and style, and I didn't sweat nearly as much as I usually did when I danced.

We won the dance contest, and somebody took a picture of us kissing on the mouth while holding our trophies. I may have felt that good two other times.

There isn't very much more to this story. I continued to make a fool of myself when I tried to talk to our sweetheart later, and she married somebody else and so did I.

But I still have my trophy and I still smile gently when I think of her, the dance contest, and the spring of 1963 when I was here, a boy of sixteen, and the azaleas were in bloom.

P.S.: Our principal passed on several years ago, so I don't think I'm going to get in any trouble for telling the part about the beer.

I'm Not Dying to Pay for My Funeral

That television commercial about preplanning your funeral has been running a lot lately. Do those people know something we don't?

Whatever, you dial 1-800-EMBALMS or some such thing,

and you plan out your funeral, paying for it in advance, of course.

The message is, if you don't make the call and get your funeral squared away while you're still among the living, you're being selfish because those you leave behind will have to bear the responsibility of seeing you off.

I don't know about anybody else, but I am not going to pick up a telephone and call some perfect stranger and talk about my funeral.

What happens if I outlive the guy I pay in advance to handle my funeral? What if he forgets to leave a note about me? I'm just as dead as ever, but now I'm out a couple of thousand and my friends and family still have a cold one on their hands.

There's a few other things, too. I'm not certain how I want my funeral to go just yet, for example. I've considered leaving enough money for a big party in my honor.

Maybe get the original Drifters to entertain with "Up on the Roof," and their other great hits.

Since there must be thirty or forty groups around calling themselves the original Drifters, it shouldn't be hard to get a booking.

Then again, maybe I'd prefer a simpler service. A few of my friends could gather and say nice things about me and there could be some soft organ music playing in the background. That would be cheaper than the party and parking wouldn't be a problem.

The other thing is, I frankly wouldn't mind being a lot of trouble after I'm gone. Let 'em scramble around trying to figure out what to do about my funeral.

I don't want to be forgotten that quickly. There was a bit of discomfort in getting me here, so there should be some hassle involved in sending me away.

One group of friends could determine what sort of funeral they want, while another could disagree.

After all, what are friends for if not to bicker among themselves? I can hear them discussing my life now:

"You know," one might say, "Lewis never handled his success very well."

"But don't forget," another might reply, "he didn't handle failure that well, either."

Go ahead and preplan your funeral and ruin all the fun that's involved in dying, but I don't want to.

Besides, all you really need to know about funerals comes from the great philosopher who once uttered, "Regardless of what you might have accomplished in life, the size of your funeral is still going to be determined by the weather."

17

LIFE
IN THE
TWENTIETH
CENTURY

How Times Have Changed

They are advertising condoms on television.

Lord, how things change.

A lot of us who grew up before there was the pill and the threat of AIDS find it hard to believe that condoms may be discussed openly.

Only men and boys—at least that's we boys thought—talked about condoms in my youth, and we talked of them only in hushed tones.

I remember the first one I ever saw. A friend of mine found one in his father's desk drawer and brought it to school. We were in the fifth grade.

We inspected it as if it were some rare find. The principal found us with the thing and took it away from us, however, and gave us a stern lecture regarding our morals and the sanctity of femalekind.

In high school, it was a measure of your manhood whether or not you had a condom on your person at all times.

Skeeter Whitlock bought one out of a machine in a rest room and put it in his wallet.

Some months later, his mother was cleaning his room and saw his wallet. There was an odd oval imprint being caused by something inside it.

Skeeter's mother looked in her son's wallet and found the condom.

"She had my dad talk to me about it," Skeeter explained later. "He told me that messing around with things like that could cut my wind and cause me not to get a football scholarship after high school. But I never really liked playing football that much in the first place."

Now that condoms may be discussed openly, you hear a lot of men my age (forty) and older remembering various experiences. Most all of us have a going-into-the-drugstore-to-buy-condoms story.

"I stood outside the drugstore for an hour trying to get up the courage to go inside," a man was saying.

"When I finally walked up and told the druggist, very quietly, what I wanted to purchase, he yelled to his assistant, 'Hey, Bob, where do we keep the rubbers?'

"I looked around and two Miss-Goody-Two-Shoes with big mouths from high school heard what he said. I ran out of the store without my purchase."

Women, we have recently learned, now account for over half the condom sales in this country, and that figure will likely go up.

Most of us never would have believed that could happen in 1960, but another acquaintance does tell this story.

"When I was a teenager, I worked in my daddy's truck stop after school. The condom salesman came by one day, and I couldn't believe it when he went into the women's rest room after going into the men's.

"When he came out, I asked, 'You mean women buy those things, too?'

" 'I got a machine in there and I get a lot of quarters out of it, but I never put no condoms in it,' he said, adding with a laugh, 'Heard any women complaining?' "

Today, he most certainly would.

Lord, how things change.

Fighting Tooth
and Nail

Normally, I'm against most anything that is supposed to be new and make my life easier.

Call waiting was new, and I came to hate it. People call me on the phone and then say, "Can you hold a minute? I've got another call."

No, I can't wait while you talk to somebody else. You called me, remember?

And who messed with the shower knobs? There used to be two knobs in the shower. One was marked C and the other was marked H.

You turned on a little C and a little H and you had yourself a nice shower. Now, however, there's something new.

There's only one knob in most showers you run into today, and Thomas Edison couldn't figure out how to keep from being scalded trying to find a comfortable water temperature in which to shower.

But I must admit I have finally found something that is new and will, in fact, improve all our lives.

I'm talking about toothpaste that now is available in a "new, neat and easy spout."

I bought some the other day. You don't squeeze the tube to make the toothpaste come out, as we have been doing as long as there has been toothpaste, I suppose.

There's a little spout at the top of the tube and all you do is press a button and out comes the toothpaste.

You can press just long enough to get a small amount of paste or you can press and get gobs.

This should help men and women get along better, as well as making brushing your teeth an entirely new experience.

One of the basic differences between men and women is that men squeeze a tube of toothpaste in a random manner. It's not a big deal to us.

Women, however, squeeze from the bottom of the tube of toothpaste first. As the bottom of the tube becomes empty, they roll that part neatly toward the top.

There are reasons for this. One, it says clearly on the tube, "For best results, squeeze from the bottom."

Women think reading a tube of toothpaste is like reading the Bible. If you don't follow the instructions on the tube, you will go to hell.

Women also think squeezing from the bottom is practicing sound economics. Squeeze from the bottom, they have been led to believe, and you get more toothpaste for your buck.

So what if you save three cents' worth of toothpaste every three months? That's twelve cents a year, which will make a nice down payment on a new condo.

Women have been complaining to men about their toothpaste habits for years, causing much friction.

But that's all in the past now. With the "new, neat and easy spout," toothpaste tubes will no longer be an issue in male and female relationships.

Now, men and women can fight and break up over more important reasons. Like leaving empty beer cans on the carpet and hanging panty hose to dry in the shower.

Special Delivery, Posthaste

Now that the post office is charging us more to mail a letter, I think the least the post office could do is offer us a few more services.

I'm quite concerned, for instance, about the fact that you can't go to the post office to mail a letter or to buy stamps without having to stand in a long line.

The only lines that are longer than the ones at the post office are those outside the ladies' room at a Willie Nelson concert and those in express lanes in grocery stores where urban terrorists attempt to sneak through with more than twelve items.

Perhaps the post office could use the extra income from the increase in stamp prices to hire more people so the lines wouldn't be so long.

Either that or they could give bonuses to postal workers who occasionally look up and notice the long lines and actually speed up to keep customers moving.

If the workers at my post office had been Pony Express riders, the Indians could have caught them on foot.

I'd also like the post office to throw out any junk mail addressed to me before it's delivered to my house.

That's all I'm going to do with it, throw it out. They know what junk mail is at the post office. They could trash anything asking me for money, for instance. That way, I'd never have to hear from any politicians or television evangelists.

I don't want to get any more mail from Ed McMahon, either. He writes me more often than my friends and relatives with that silly business about the sweepstakes I know I'm not going to win.

And speaking of relatives, I wouldn't mind the post office going through letters from my kin, either, and throwing out those I get from my Aunt Gloria.

Aunt Gloria is a sweet lady and I love her, but all her letters start the same way: "You're not going to believe what the doctors found Thursday. . . ."

What then follows is a detailed discussion of how her various bodily parts are in horrid states of disrepair, and how, if I don't eat a lot of prunes, stay out of the night air, and take oatmeal baths, the same sorts of things could happen to me.

These letters leave me terribly depressed. The post office could simply call me on the phone and say, "Your aunt Gloria wrote you again," and that would alert me she is thinking of me, but I wouldn't have to read of any anatomical catastrophes.

The post office also could do a better job with my bills. Have you ever noticed how all your bills come on the same day? The post office could send your bills one at a time, enabling you to avoid financial panic.

The post office could call and ask, "When would you like your credit-card bill?"

"How much is it?"

"A lot."

"Don't send it until next week. I should be over the electric bill you sent me yesterday by then."

Let's see Federal Express top that.

Mebbe the Front Porch Should Come Back

I was driving through the outskirts of the city the other day and I saw a man sitting on a front porch.

It was an older house and he was an older man. Modern houses don't have front porches anymore, and even if they did, younger men have far too much to do to sit on them.

I'm not certain when the front porch all but disappeared from American life, but it probably was about the same time television and air-conditioning were being installed in most every home.

Why sit out on the porch where it's hot and you can get mosquito-bit when you can sit inside where it's comfort-cooled and watch *Ozzie and Harriet?*

Even if an architect designs a porch today, it's usually placed in the back of the house where the hot tub is.

If we do venture out of our houses today, it's usually to get in the hot tub.

If Americans continue to spend all that time in their hot tubs, we may all eventually shrink down like the Lilliputians and become prunelike from boiling ourselves one too many times.

I grew up in my grandparents' home. They had a front porch; we spent a lot of time sitting on it.

My grandmother would shell butter beans. My grandfather would listen for trains.

"There comes the mail train to Montgomery," he'd say, pulling his watch out of his watch pocket. "She's running four minutes late."

I learned a lot sitting on the front porch with my grandparents. How to shell butter beans. How to find the Big Dipper. How to wait for a mosquito to alight and then slap that sucker dead. What a pleasure it is to listen for trains.

Our neighbors often dropped by and sat on the porch with us.

"It was awful what happened to Norvell Tenny, wasn't it?" a neighbor would say.

"What happened to him?" my grandmother would ask, looking up from her butter beans.

"Got three fingers cut clean off down at the sawmill."

Something else I learned on the front porch—not to include sawmilling in my future.

But even my grandparents eventually moved inside. They bought a television and enclosed the front porch and made it a den.

My grandfather enjoyed westerns. My grandmother never missed a Billy Graham sermon or a televised wrestling match. The mail train to Montgomery had to get along by itself after that.

Perhaps if front porches came back and people started sitting on them again, we'd learn to relax more and talk to one another more, and being bitten by a mosquito would at least be some contact with nature.

I probably should have stopped and talked to the old man on the porch and gotten his opinions on all of this.

I would have, too, but I was late for my tee time.

How to Be a
Clock-Eyed Manager

There was a study released by Priority Management Corporation of Pittsburgh regarding how much time the average American spends during a lifetime doing such activities as waiting in line and waiting at a red light.

The study, according to *USA Today*, indicated we spend an average of five years waiting in lines and six months sitting at red lights.

There were other such findings regarding how much time we devote to life's functions. We spend:

- Eight months opening junk mail
- Three years attending meetings
- Four years doing housework
- Six years eating
- One year searching for lost possessions

After reading all this, I began to think about my own life and how much time I spend at certain activities. Perhaps, I thought to myself, this endeavor would allow me to manage my own time a little better.

- *Eating and waiting in line:*   I put these two together because I probably wouldn't spend nearly as much time eating as other Americans if I didn't order from drive-thrus at fast-food places so often where you wait in line thirty minutes to get a hamburger it took ninety seconds to cook.

- *Housework:* I don't do much housework. I scrape green stuff off the plates that have been sitting in my sink for a couple of weeks, but that's about it. Leave that green stuff unchecked for too long, somebody told me, and it can flat take over your house.
- *Opening junk mail:* I don't spend very much time with junk mail, either. I especially hate those silly letters I get from American Express. It's like I told the guy who called about my American Express bill: "Hey, Jack, if I had money to pay my bills I wouldn't need your credit card."
- *Searching for lost possessions:* I'll probably spend fifteen years of my life doing that. I can never locate my watch, my wallet, my glasses, or the remote-control device for the television.

The other day, I found my watch in the kitchen sink (with a lot of green stuff on it), my wallet in the icebox, my glasses in a Holiday Inn near Paducah, Kentucky, and the remote-control device for my television in the trunk of my car.

How these items found their way to such exotic places, I'll never know. Perhaps it was the work of fairies.

- *Attending meetings:* I don't spend the same amount of time attending meetings as the average American does. I was afraid if I remained in the Rotary Club much longer, that food would kill me.
- *What else:* I figure I've spent seven years of my life waiting for women to come out of ladies' rooms, eleven years receiving unsolicited advice, eight years watching television (as long as I can still get the Playboy Channel on cable and continue to locate my remote-control device), and two years sitting in traffic.

Add all that to the time I'll spend sleeping, and that only gives me a few days left to worry about whether or not the earth is going to get so hot it will burn up.

Priority time management. It works for me.

Gone With the Wind

For years now, I have been encouraged to produce my column on a computer.

"It's so much easier on a computer," people say. "You can move things around and edit and insert without any trouble."

I have resisted, however, and this is coming to you, as always, from my 1953 Royal manual.

There are a few problems with my typewriter. The e character falls off its arm occasionally, for instance. In fact, I once wrote an entire book with no e's.

"What are these blank spaces?" asked my editor when I turned in the manuscript.

"Everywhere you see a blank space," I said, "put in an e."

My editor enjoyed that. It gave him something to do and it made him feel worthwhile.

What I really worry about when I think of writing something on a computer is, where does all that writing go when you push a button and it vanishes from the screen?

Is it kept in a batch of wires in the back of the computer? Does it go to some central location in a vault buried underneath a K mart in Fort Wayne, Indiana?

And what else I've always wondered is, what guarantee do

I have that when all my work disappears from that screen, it will come back when I summon it?

"Don't worry," say computer types, "it can't be lost."

Right.

The *Titanic* couldn't sink. Liston couldn't lose to Clay. Dewey was going to beat the stuffings out of Truman. And Star Wars will work.

Did you hear what happened to the keynote speaker for the Democratic Convention?

Ann Richards, Texas state treasurer, was working with speechwriter John Sherman.

Mr. Sherman had completed a rough draft of the speech and had stored it in his computer.

But when he hit the print command on his magic box, only one page came out. The rest had disappeared into that black void out there.

Mr. Sherman even called in a technician, but he couldn't bring back the speech, either. So Sherman had to write the blamed thing over again.

What if Margaret Mitchell had written *Gone With the Wind* on a computer, and when she tried to call it back, it wouldn't come?

Do you think Margaret Mitchell would have written the whole thing over again?

Of course not. She would have taken a hammer to her computer and then gone into another line of work, and we'd never have known about Rhett and Scarlett.

What about other great pieces of writing? The United States Constitution, for instance.

Ben Franklin calls Thomas Jefferson and says, "Tom, send me over a copy of the Constitution."

"Sorry, Ben," Jefferson would answer. "I stored it in my computer, but now I can't find it anymore."

They would have been scrambling around trying to put the Constitution back together again and might have missed important stuff like freedom of assembly and it might have been against the law even to have political conventions, which might not have been a bad idea, but let us leave that for another time. I'm flat out of typing paper anyway.

Horses Drive
Me Buggy

Some fool tried to get me to go horseback riding the other day. I was visiting friends and they own a lot of land and they've got dogs and cats and cows and even a few chickens.

I'm not certain how many horses they have, but there appeared to be enough to refilm a couple of episodes of *F Troop.*

I not only said no to the invitation to climb upon a horse, but I added a familiar expletive in front of it so there would be no misunderstanding as to the strength of my resolve.

"Then stay here and pet the dogs," I was told, and everybody went out to ride.

My dislike for horseback riding goes way back.

My uncle was a farmer and he grew corn. When I was a small boy, he offered me gainful employment as a corn puller one chilly Saturday afternoon.

Since I needed a few coins for a trip to town to see a movie, I took my uncle up on his proposal.

I don't know how many out there have ever had the opportunity to pull ears of corn from their stalks, but if you haven't, decline any and all offers to do so.

Ears of corn do not come off their stalks without a fight. I twisted and pulled ears of corn for eight hours, and when we were done, I expected payment for my efforts.

"You did a good job today," my uncle said. "You can ride my horse any time you want to."

I tried to call the Child Labor Abuse Office and turn in my uncle, but my mother wouldn't let me.

"Why don't you ride the horse?" she suggested.

What the heck. As I stood while my uncle saddled his horse, the horse stepped on my toe.

I threatened a lawsuit and vowed never again to get near a horse I didn't have money on.

I kept my vow for thirty years. Then I was vacationing out West and my companion said, "Let's go horseback riding."

My horse was named Leatherneck. Hers was Colonel.

"These horses must have been in a war with names like that," my companion said.

"The Spanish–American from the looks of them," I said.

I followed her and Colonel, who turned out to have a serious gas problem.

"Can't you keep up?" she asked, as I pulled Leatherneck back several lengths.

"Either you turn that horse around and make him go backward, or I'm sticking back here," I said. "My olfactory system can't take any more."

One other thing. Nobody told me you ought to wear socks when you ride a horse or the stirrups will cut through your ankles and cause you much pain.

My ankles are still bearing scars of the last time I rode a horse, which was the last time I'll ever ride a horse.

God gave us Henry Ford and cabfare for some reason, and now I know what it was.

How to Treat a Lady

I was entering a building recently and a lady walked up behind me.

I opened the door, stood back, and allowed the lady to go first. She smiled and said, "Thank you."

I followed behind her and we came upon another door. I waited for her to go ahead.

But she just stood there. For a moment, I was puzzled at her delay. Then it occurred to me. She was waiting for me to open the door for her again, which I promptly did. Again she smiled and said, "Thank you."

How refreshing. It had been a long time since I have run across a woman—and a fairly young one at that—who seemed to want and expect a bit of chivalry from the opposite sex.

I think I can speak for most American men and say we are terribly confused in this day of liberated women. We're not sure if women want us to treat them in the old, mannerly way or not.

If I open a door for a woman, will she take it to mean I think she's not strong enough to open it herself and knee me in the groin?

Judging from the incident I described above, there may be, in fact, a number of women out there who still do appreciate a bit of gallantry now and then.

I realize I might be a bit rusty in this area, so what I did was ask around among my female acquaintances until I found one from the old school who could reprogram me a bit on how to treat a lady.

"Do you know," she began, "how to handle it when you approach a revolving door with a woman by your side?"

I had no clue.

"You go first," she explained, "and push the door so the lady can simply walk behind you without having to put out any effort of her own."

There were others:

- Walking on the sidewalk. "A man should always walk nearest the curb, in case a car might come along and splash water."
- Lighting a cigarette. "Not that many people smoke anymore, but in case you meet a lady who does, it is quite appropriate to light her cigarette. If you both are smoking, light hers first if you have a lighter. If you are using a match, it is appropriate for the man to light his first, so as to take the noxious fumes that erupt when a match is first struck."
- Standing when a lady enters the room. "I still appreciate that. It makes me feel special."
- Helping a lady out of a car. "Offer her one hand and then put the other gently behind her back. Never put both hands on her."
- On elevators. "When leaving an elevator, if it is not crowded, stand aside and allow the woman to walk out first."

I had just one more question:

"What if I follow all those rules but run into a woman who is offended by them, and she knees me in the groin?"

"Once you catch your breath," said my friend, "tip your hat and offer her a cigar."

Thingamabobs and Whatchamacallits

Another Christmas, another bunch of gadget gifts from my relatives and friends.

I'm not certain why I always get gadgets for Christmas, but it might have to do with the fact my relatives and friends consider me to be a helpless person.

Otherwise, why would anybody give me a device that is supposed to make flossing my teeth less complicated?

I'll admit I'm still not sure which fingers to wrap the floss around, but I eventually would have figured it out.

However, I now have this thing that looks sort of like a slingshot, and you wrap the floss around it and there's a handle.

So now I don't have to remember which fingers to use when I'm flossing, and if I ever needed to go out and kill a squirrel for dinner, I suppose I could load up my flosser with a couple of rocks and go stalk around some trees until I've found my prey.

And speaking of food, I suppose my friends and relatives think I don't know where any good seafood restaurants are, either.

I got a pocket fisherman this year. I suppose if I can't kill any squirrels with my flosser, and if I happen to be passing any major bodies of water, I could park my car and take my pocket fisherman out of my pocket and cast for a few fried flounders or blackened redfish.

I almost forgot about the automatic toothbrush I got to go with my flosser.

You plug it into the wall, put it into your mouth, and the automatic toothbrush does the rest.

At first, I had a problem with my automatic toothbrusher. I'd put toothpaste on it, switch it on, and it made these violent motions that would spray the toothpaste all over the room.

I told the person who gave me the gift about the problem I was having with it.

"What you have to do is put the toothbrush in your mouth before you switch it on," she explained. "That way you don't spray the toothpaste all over the bathroom."

I would have figured that out eventually, too.

I also received a device that will give me hot lather with which to shave.

It sits there with my flosser and my automatic toothbrush, and I plug it into the wall and I've got hot lather.

The neighbors will probably find out about this and will always be over asking, "May I borrow a cup of hot lather?"— especially the newlyweds across the street, who are into reading the letters to *Penthouse.*

I also received a radio for my shower this Christmas. So I can keep up on any late-breaking news while I'm washing between my toes.

I also received an electric shoe-horn, another thing that follows me around to see where I put my car keys and then tells me where they are when I forget where I put them, a mechanical banana peeler, a partridge in a pear tree that gives the time and can be used as a lamp, a security system that goes under my bed and sounds off if there's a three-eyed monster under there, and another beeper that goes off if I walk outside my house having neglected to zip my fly.

All I didn't get that I needed was a machine that's smart enough to figure out how the VCR I bought works.

Maybe next year.

Life in the Year 2000

Ever since the 1980's began, I've been counting down to the new century.

According to my latest calculations, the year 2000 should be here in slightly less than twelve more years.

I don't know about anybody else, but I am glad I've got a shot at living to see a turn of the century.

According to further calculations, there's only been nineteen of those so far. Not everybody gets a chance to witness such a momentous occasion.

If I make it to 2000, I'll be fifty-three. That's not nearly as old as I once thought it was. I might still have enough left in me by then to throw a giant turn-of-the-century party at my condo on the moon, where some developer no doubt will have built a golf course.

I've also been considering what problems we might encounter when the new century arrives.

I can't think of how we're going to say "2000" in regard, say, to the World Series.

This year we will say, "Welcome to the 1989 World Series."

Somehow, however, I can't come to grips with "Welcome to the 2000 World Series."

It seems awkward and cumbersome to say that, and the only other time there was such a problem was in the year 1000, when there was no baseball.

And think about checks. All our lives, we would have written checks with the little "19" up where you fill in the year in which you are writing the check.

Twelve years from now, you'll pull out a check and there will be a little "20" up there in the corner.

Then, again, there probably won't be any checks by the year 2000. You'll have your own computer that is hooked into the bank and you'll simply punch in the amount of your withdrawal and the bank will put your money in a tube that leads directly to your house.

The only real problem will be learning to count in yen.

Think of the state of things by the year 2000.

- Somebody will have figured out by then how to make a commercial airliner go five thousand miles per hour. Of course, it will still take forty-five minutes to get the plane from its gate to its takeoff position.
- It will have been determined that heavy exercise, like jogging and aerobics, causes flat feet, hepatitis, and acne.
- *The Wall Street Journal* will have run a photo on page one; and *USA Today* will have printed an article with more than eleven sentences—three compound.
- Dentists will have figured out how to fill your teeth using a laser beam rather than a drill. It will cost twenty-seven times more to have a tooth filled, nullifying any loss of pain.
- McDonald's will be selling goat sandwiches.
- Everybody will have seen every episode of *M*A*S*H* six hundred times.
- The federal deficit will be so large by then, we will have to sell off North Dakota, Montana, and that silly-looking top part of Idaho to the Canadians.
- Dogs will be able to talk. They will say, "I've always enjoyed Alpo, but it gives me gas."
- Elvis will still be dead.
- So will the Atlanta Falcons.

About the Author

In the last eleven years, LEWIS GRIZZARD has produced eleven national best-sellers, including *Don't Bend over in the Garden, Granny, You Know Them Taters Got Eyes; When My Love Returns from the Ladies Room, Will I Be Too Old to Care?; My Daddy Was a Pistol and I'm a Son of a Gun; Shoot Low, Boys—They're Ridin' Shetland Ponies;* and *Elvis Is Dead and I Don't Feel So Good Myself.* His home paper is the *Atlanta Journal-Constitution,* and he is syndicated in more than four hundred newspapers nationwide. He lives in Atlanta.